W9-BNN-526

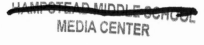
DEMCO

Hispanic Heritage

Hispanic Heritage

Title List

Central American Immigrants to the United States: Refugees from Unrest

Cuban Americans: Exiles from an Island Home

First Encounters Between Spain and the Americas: Two Worlds Meet

Latino Americans and Immigration Laws: Crossing the Border

Latino Americans in Sports, Film, Music, and Government: Trailblazers

Latino Arts and Their Influence on the United States: Songs, Dreams, and Dances

Latino Cuisine and Its Influence on American Foods: The Taste of Celebration

Latino Economics in the United States: Job Diversity

Latino Folklore and Culture: Stories of Family, Traditions of Pride

Latino Migrant Workers: America's Harvesters

Latinos Today: Facts and Figures

The Latino Religious Experience: People of Faith and Vision

Mexican Americans' Role in the United States: A History of Pride, A Future of Hope

Puerto Ricans' History and Promise: Americans Who Cannot Vote

South America's Immigrants to the United States: The Flight from Turmoil

The Story of Latino Civil Rights: Fighting for Justice

First Encounters Between Spain and the Americas

Two Worlds Meet

by Kenneth McIntosh

Mason Crest Publishers

Philadelphia

Mason Crest Publishers Inc.

370 Reed Road

Broomall, Pennsylvania 19008

(866) MCP-BOOK (toll free)

First printing

1 2 3 4 5 6 7 8 9 10

           Library of Congress Cataloging-in-Publication Data

McIntosh, Kenneth, 1959-

  First encounters between Spain and the Americas : two worlds meet / by Kenneth
McIntosh.

     p. cm. —— (Hispanic heritage)

Includes bibliographical references and index.

 ISBN 1-59084-925-6 ISBN 1-59084-924-8 (series)

 1. America—Discovery and exploration—Spanish—Juvenile literature. 2.—Spain—
Colonies—America—History—Juvenile literature. 3. Spaniards—America—History—
Juvenile literature. 4. America Colonization—Juvenile literature. 5. Indians—First
contact with Europeans—Juvenile literature. 6. Indians, Treatment of—Juvenile literature. 7. Culture conflict—America—History—Juvenile literature. I. Title. II. Hispanic
heritage (Philadelphia, Pa.)

 E123.M376 2005

 970.01'6——dc22

                               2004017788

Produced by Harding House Publishing Service, Inc., Vestal, NY.
Interior design by Dianne Hodack and MK Bassett-Harvey.
Cover design by Dianne Hodack.
Printed and bound in the Hashemite Kingdom of Jordan.

Contents

Introduction

by José E. Limón, Ph.D.

ven before there was a United States, Hispanics were present in what would become this country. Beginning in the sixteenth century, Spanish explorers traversed North America, and their explorations encouraged settlement as early as the sixteenth century in what is now northern New Mexico and Florida, and as late as the mid-eighteenth century in what is now southern Texas and California.

Later, in the nineteenth century, following Spain's gradual withdrawal from the New World, Mexico in particular established its own distinctive presence in what is now the southwestern part of the United States, a presence reinforced in the first half of the twentieth century by substantial immigration from that country. At the close of the nineteenth century, the U.S. war with Spain brought Cuba and Puerto Rico into an interactive relationship with the United States, the latter in a special political and economic affiliation with the United States even as American power influenced the course of almost every other Latin American country.

The books in this series remind us of these historical origins, even as each explores the present reality of different Hispanic groups. Some of these books explore the contemporary social origins—what social scientists call the "push" factors—behind the accelerating Hispanic immigration to America: political instability, economic underdevelopment and crisis, environmental degradation, impoverished or wholly absent educational systems, and other circumstances contribute to many Latin Americans deciding they will be better off in the United States.

And, for the most part, they will be. The vast majority come to work and work very hard, in order to earn better wages than they would back home. They fill significant labor needs in the U.S. economy and contribute to the economy through lower consumer prices and sales taxes.

When they leave their home countries, many immigrants may initially fear that they are leaving behind vital and important aspects of their home cultures: the Spanish language, kinship ties, food, music, folklore, and the arts. But as these books also make clear, culture is a fluid thing, and these native cultures are not only brought to America, they are also replenished in the United States in fascinating and novel ways. These books further suggest to us that Hispanic groups enhance American culture as a whole.

Our country—especially the young, future leaders who will read these books—can only benefit by the fair and full knowledge these authors provide about the socio-historical origins and contemporary cultural manifestations of America's Hispanic heritage.

1

Center of the World

Proud of itself is the city of Mexico—Tenochtitlan

Here no one fears to die in war.

This is our glory.

This is your command,

Oh Giver of life!

Have this in mind, oh princes,

Do not forget it.

Who could conquer Tenochtitlan?

Who could shake the foundations of heaven?

—an ancient Mexican poem

Artwork

A street mural in Los Angeles portrays some of the earliest Americans.

Moctezuma the Second was Huey Tlatoani (ruler) of Tenochtitlan (Te-noch-teet-lan), the center of the great Aztec Empire and the center of the world (at least from Moctezuma's perspective). Yet despite his power, Moctezuma was uneasy as he stood alone on the balcony of his palace.

The sun, visible image of the mighty god Huitzilopochtli (Weet-zeel-oh-potch-ly), had nearly completed its journey across the sky. A cool breeze tugged at the feathered fringe of the scarlet cotton cape across Moctezuma's shoulders. In his right hand he held a warm drink of frothy chocolate, steaming in its gold cup. In his other hand he held a burning tobacco stick, wrapped in aromatic leaves. The smoke and drink warmed his insides, but they could not settle the chill he felt in his spirit.

The ruler's keen eyes gazed across his mighty city. Tenochtitlan was indeed blessed by the gods. Built with incredible effort right in the middle of a lake, at the place chosen by Huitzilopochtli, it was home to 300,000 people. From the great salt water in the East to the great salt water in the West, and from the desert lands many days journey north to the tropical jungles of the Mayan tribes in the south, millions of people obeyed orders sent from Tenochtitlan. Yet Moctezuma was not at peace.

He gazed across a bridge-road toward the marketplace of Tlatelolco. Tens of thousands of people were still busy bartering, even as the business day drew to its close. The streets were full of artists, selling finely worked vessels of gold, silver, and copper. Woven capes and shawls of exquisite quetzal bird feathers, fine jewelry of jade and turquoise, all exchanged hands in the bazaars. Jaguar skins, glassy obsidian stones, copal resin for incense, and other

Statue of Moctezuma

precious trade goods were for sale in abundance, for those wealthy enough to buy them. Weavers sold bolts of brilliantly dyed cloth to tailors and others who would cut and shape them into fashionable outfits. Fresh foods were carried by swift runners' feet from throughout the empire. These included all manner of fish from lakes and both oceans, turkeys, quail, ducks and partridge, rabbits, deer and other game, along with vast quantities of corn, every kind of vegetable, and piles of fresh baked tortillas and tamales. There were jars full of pulque (fermented maguey cactus juice). Even the poorest Mexicas could live without hunger in this place of plenty. Nonetheless, Moctezuma still felt a small emptiness inside.

His mind traveled from his sight to the vast empire beyond. He could not even recall all the tribes and villages that had sworn their loyalty to him. Many had chosen to join the Mexica willingly, seeing the advantages they gained in trade and protection. Others had resisted Mexica rule.

Moctezuma thought of his elite troops, the jaguar and eagle warriors. All Mexica males were soldiers when called on, but these noble regiments were professional warriors. They dressed from head to foot in brilliant skins and feathers, and were armed with razor-sharp obsidian-edged swords, along with throwing sticks and lethal darts. No known tribe could resist an onslaught of Mexica armies. Those who did not serve the empire out of genuine loyalty learned to serve, eventually, out of fear.

Why, then, did the lord of the Mexicas feel a tinge of worry in his belly?

His gaze returned to the city before him. He could see tiny figures, like ants scrambling over a vast anthill: priests cleaning blood off the steps of the Templo Mayor. This vast pyramid, home to the gods Tlaloc and Huitzilopochtli, was the very heart of Tenochtitlan. It was here, atop the gleaming white mountain of stone, that the vast and terrible forces of the natural world were kept in balance. The gods had created humankind by giving their own blood. To have energy for their work—traveling across the sky, bringing forth crops upon the earth—the deities required great amounts of food. Captured enemies and sometimes specially chosen Mexicas were fed to the gods in the sacred precinct. It was demanding work, providing the thousands of human hearts the gods required on an annual basis, but the Mexicas took seriously their responsibility to keep the divine powers well satisfied. Yet Moctezuma wondered . . . was there some deity they had, of late, failed to please?

In a few more minutes, his servants would come and politely inform him it was time for dinner. Small crowds of officials, family members, and visiting leaders from villages throughout the empire would sit on soft reed mats and sample hundreds of different dishes of carefully prepared food. Musicians, comedians, and dancers would entertain him and his guests. A host of slaves would rush in and out of the kitchens and washrooms of the palace, making sure the guests were at all times well served. This was not an unusual dinner—special festivals would be far more magnificent—but Moctezuma's ordinary meals were lavish enough that visiting guests would tell stories about their meals for days afterward.

Despite all the glories of his empire, Moctezuma knew the Aztec world sat upon a shaky foundation. The forces of the natural world—rain and sun, crops and animal life—could easily go out of balance. When that happened, even the strongest mortals need fear. And in the past week, there had been signs that the universe might indeed have become unstable.

Arising at night to go to the bathroom, a young priest of Huitzilopochtli had seen a comet, "bleeding like a terrible wound, spilling out fire, across the sky." The next night, all the Mexicas stood outside their homes, gazing at the fearful sign blazing across the heavens. Such an omen, occurring at an unlucky time in the calendar, signaled something was wrong in the world of the gods.

Moctezuma

Then messengers had brought strange and troubling news. Strangers, white-skinned and dressed in shining metal from head to foot, had appeared on the coast, coming in enormous canoes. They rode on enormous deer and had power to throw lightning that destroyed whatever it touched. They were traveling toward Tenochtitlan. Were they a new tribe of men, unseen before? Were they spirit beings from the supernatural world? Did they mean good or ill for the Mexicas?

Moctezuma thought of all these things, and was troubled.

The comet that foretold changes to come

The Western Hemisphere

ooking from outer space, we all inhabit an enormous blue sphere—our earth. If we divide this globe by cutting it in

The Western Hemisphere is on the left, the Eastern on the right.

half from top to bottom, we can imagine hemispheres. ("Hemi" means half, and a sphere is round, so a hemisphere is half of something round, in this case, the globe.) The Eastern Hemisphere contains Africa, Australia, Europe, and Asia. People who come from this part of the world sometimes call it the "Old World." The Western Hemisphere consists of what we today call the "Americas." Once they became aware of it, people in the Eastern Hemisphere called the Western Hemisphere the "New World." Yet it was hardly new to the millions of people who had lived there for thousands of years.

Today, we have given labels to the Western Hemisphere based on political divisions. To the north is Alaska, part of the United States of America. Below that is Canada, then the United States. Below that is Mexico. Mexico is more than 700,000 square miles in size and home to more than 101 million people. These three nations—Canada, the United States, and Mexico—are all part of the continent we call North America.

Mexico, though geographically part of North America, is also part of Latin America. Latin America refers to the nations that begin with Mexico and reach to the southern tip of South America, nations that were colonized by Spanish-speaking Europeans. Latin America covers more than 8 million square miles.

South of North America is a narrow section of land called Central America, or Mesoamerica. Lying a little above the equator, these countries are said to experience "eternal spring." Below Mesoamerica, we come to South America, covering 6,878,000 miles. As you travel below the equator, seasons become the opposite of what they are north of the equator. So, if it is freezing cold winter in Canada, it is sunny summertime down in Argentina. The Caribbean Islands

hen Europeans reached Tenochtitlan, they were astonished at its size and population. With approximately 300,000 inhabitants, it was bigger than the largest city in Spain—Seville—which claimed 60,000 residents. London, at that time, had only 50,000 citizens. Paris and Constantinople were the only cities in the world that may have had as many people as the Mexica capital. Today, Mexico City is the third largest in the world, with 18 million people. Moctezuma would be pleased to see that his city still ranks among the greatest.

are also part of the Western Hemisphere. Caribbean nations include Cuba, the Dominican Republic, Haiti, and Puerto Rico.

The First Inhabitants
of the Western Hemisphere

ho discovered this vast Western Hemisphere? Which direction did they come from? No one today knows. They came at least 15,000 years ago. Until recently, sci-

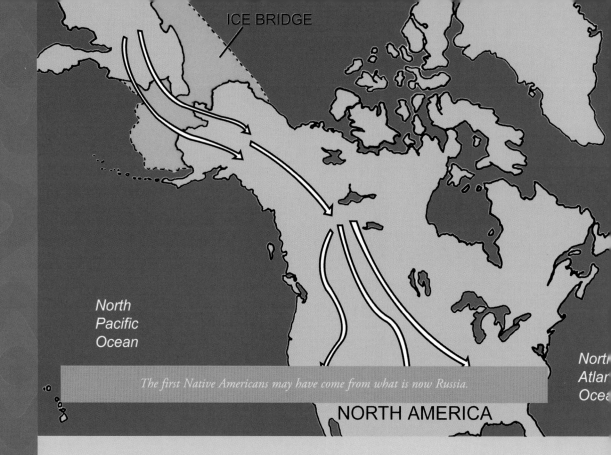

ICE BRIDGE

North
Pacific
Ocean

The first Native Americans may have come from what is now Russia.

NORTH AMERICA

Nort
Atlar
Ocea

entists felt certain people walked from Asia into North America over a land bridge that temporarily connected those continents. They were mammoth hunters, dressing in warm skins and following herds of enormous mammals for their food. According to this theory, they walked from north to south until they had spread out over the entirety of North, Central, and South America.

Recently, this land bridge theory has been thrown into doubt. Some of the most ancient yet most advanced prehistoric cultures have been found in the extreme south of South America. If *migration* went north to south, how did people get south first? Archaeologists now wonder whether prehistoric people came to America by boat or by foot, from north or from south, or if different groups of people arrived different ways simultaneously. Some Native people say they *originated* in the Americas. We may never be able to prove how, when, or why the first people came to this part of our earth.

We do know that when Europeans arrived, the Western Hemisphere was already home to hundreds of cultures, with a vast variety of languages, customs, and spiritual beliefs. Scholars estimate between 40 and 90 million people inhabited the Americas before

Columbus arrived. In what is today called Latin America, there were three great empires—the Aztec, Maya, and Inca.

The Aztec

migration: the movement from one place to another.

originated: began.

Mexico is named after the Mexica, who between A.D. 1200 and 1500 united that land into a mighty empire. All the tribes that formed this empire were together known as "Aztecs." The Mexica came from a place they called Aztlán, in what is today the southwestern United States. They gained in strength and military power over centuries of migration. Their leaders were called Tlatoani, which means "speaker," and the supreme leader of the Mexicas was called the Huey Tlatoani.

In 1325, following a vision given by Huitzilopochtli, the Mexicas arrived at a lake where an eagle, with a writhing snake in its beak, sat atop a cactus. This was to be the site of their capital, Tenochtitlan. From here, they conquered and ruled neighboring tribes.

The eagle perched on a cactus with a serpent in its mouth

The Maya

The Mayan people lived in Mesoamerica. Between A.D. 250 and 900, the Maya developed an advanced civilization. They had a 365-day calendar, invented the concept of zero in numbers, had a form of writing, and built enormous cities centered around great pyramids and temples. Their capital, Tikal, housed more than 10,000 people in a magnificent city.

Around A.D. 800, the Mayan population reached the point where lack of adequate food, political disagreements, and warfare among themselves forced them to leave their beautiful cities. When Europeans arrived centuries later, the Mayan people were living in small villages, as many of them still do.

The Inca

 n Peru, people who called themselves Runa developed a mighty empire. Their society was built around a king, known as "the Inca," who was regarded as the descendant of supernatural heroes. The entire Runa Empire became known by the name of their ruler, so they were called "Inca." From 1438 to 1532, the Inca expanded their empire, and the Inca's capital, Cuzco, was an architectural wonder. Master mathematicians, the Runa, used a decimal system to organize their vast empire into units of tens, hundreds, and thousands. They carved enormous pictures of giant creatures—spiders, jaguars, and so on—on the Nazca plains. These drawings, still visible today, are so large they can only be seen from the sky. Machu Picchu, a mountain fortress where the Inca retreated after the Europeans came, continues to amaze tourists who travel from around the world to see it. Today in Peru, many of the Inca's descendants continue to speak their ancestral language, Quechua.

National Symbol

After centuries of wandering, the Mexica's migration came to an end when they saw a prickly cactus pear growing on an island in the middle of Lake Texcoco. Upon it was a great eagle, with a snake in its mouth. This was the exact sign the god Huitzilopochtli had said would mark their permanent home. Today, the eagle and cactus are the national symbols of the Republic of Mexico.

Ancient Spirituality

The Aztecs, Inca, and Maya were all deeply spiritual people. Enormous pyramids, breathtaking artwork, and complex ceremonies grew around their religious beliefs. Spirit beings—most often referred to as gods in modern writing—governed the natural world. The stars, the sun and moon, and natural substances such as flint, corn, and Mother Earth were the visible forms that represented these deities.

One aspect of their faith was human sacrifice. Scholars today disagree over what really took place, and it is an emotional and controversial subject. The Inca and Maya practiced human sacrifice in limited ways, but the Aztecs did so on a larger scale. The Mexica

The first encounter between Spain and North America

believed such sacrifices were necessary for spiritual reasons: spirit beings that ran the universe needed blood to keep up their strength.

The Meeting of Two Worlds

Moctezuma had reason to be unsettled, even as he gazed out on the splendor of the Mexica Empire. He could not have imagined the catastrophe about to befall his people. For more than 15,000 years, the cultures of the Western Hemisphere had flourished. In all this time, the Eastern and Western halves of planet Earth had lived in blissful ignorance of each other's existence. Now, suddenly, two worlds were about to meet.

Contributions

     he Mexica, Maya, and Inca made many lasting contributions to today's world. They cultivated potatoes, beans, and corn. North America's favorite sport—basketball—comes from the rubber-ball game played by the Aztecs and Maya. Medicines first discovered by native people in the Western Hemisphere are used daily to cure serious illnesses. Cultural practices, place names, and national identities throughout Latin America come from Mexica, Mayan, and Incan roots.

Habla Español

Las tres Américas (las trace ah-mare-ee-cahs): the three Americas

América del Norte (ah-mare-ee-cah dale nore-tay): North America

América Central (ah-mare-ee-cah sane-trahl): Central America

América del Sur (ah-mare-ee-cah dale soor): South America

2

Castile

O King Don Fernando and Doña Isabella,
With you the Golden Years begin.
—Juan del Encina, 1495

Artwork The painting's symbolism portrays the fruitfulness of King Ferdinand and Queen Isabella's reign.

"God, save me from this dishonorable marriage—either kill me, or else kill my enemy before he captures me!" By candlelight, in her darkened chamber, sixteen-year-old Princess Isabella of Castile prayed out loud. Her face was stained with tears, and her eyes were swollen from crying. She had not eaten or slept for more than a day.

"Do not worry, *mi Princesa*. God will not allow you to marry the Master of Calatrava. Look! I have a dagger. If he should enter the castle, I myself will plunge it into his heart." Isabella's lady-in-waiting, Beatriz de Bobadilla, tried to calm her mistress, but Isabella continued to weep and pray.

Struggle for a Kingdom

n the year 1467, Isabella was one of three siblings caught up in the struggle for Castile. Castile was the largest kingdom in the Iberian Peninsula. The Iberian Peninsula straddles the Mediterranean Sea and Atlantic Ocean and lies between Europe and Africa, so it is important for control of these waterways and continents. Muslims held Granada, on the southern shore of the peninsula. In centuries past, the majority of the Iberian Peninsula's population had been Muslim. Over time, the Christian kingdoms of Castile, Aragon, and Portugal had pushed Islamic forces back toward the Mediterranean. At the same time, the Christian kingdoms warred among themselves.

Isabella's half-brother, Henry IV, was King of Castile. The rebels fighting against Henry wanted to place Isabella's younger brother, Prince Alfonso, on the throne. The Master of Calatrava was a powerful knight who promised to help Henry win, but on

Isabella was held in a medieval castle like this one.

one condition—he wanted to marry Isabella. So Henry held his half-sister in a castle where he would force her to marry the Master as soon as he arrived.

Isabella hated the Master of Calatrava—he was a *lecherous* man who had made passes at her mother. Isabella was noted for intelligence, strong will, and faith in God. Her prayers apparently paid off—the Master of Calatrava suddenly became sick and died on the way to her castle.

Isabella soon joined the forces of her brother Alfonso. After Alfonso died, the rebel troops made her their leader. Isabella knew the brutal war was harming Castile, so she made a deal with Henry: "Declare me heir to the throne and we will make peace."
He agreed.

An Important Marriage

n 1469, Isabella heard of a more attractive chance at marriage. Prince Ferdinand was heir to the throne of the neighboring kingdom of Aragon. He was "handsome in face,

Ferdinand and Isabella

body and person," known for breaking a few hearts and fighting valiantly in battle. Ferdinand's father, the King of Aragon, was thrilled at the idea of his son marrying into the royal family of Castile, since that kingdom was much larger than his.

The marriage seemed like a good idea—but not to Isabella's old foe, her half-brother Henry. When Henry heard Isabella might marry Ferdinand, he was enraged. Aragon had long been his enemy. Henry ordered troops to prevent Ferdinand from meeting Isabella. The Prince of Aragon, clever as he was courageous, sneaked into the kingdom in disguise. With the help of the Archbishop of Toledo, Ferdinand and Isabella eloped.

Their marriage made history. By uniting Castile and Aragon, they created the nation known today as Spain. The newly united Spanish nation became a world superpower. Poets and *troubadours* declared it was a new "Golden Age."

In the Middle Ages, queens were expected to look nice beside their ruling husbands—and not do much more. Isabella changed that. She retained full control over Castile, even as Ferdinand ruled over Aragon. Their motto was "Tanto Monta," "Each is as good as the other." Isabella was well educated, and she used her knowledge of classical law to alter the political system of Spain. She gave the royal couple more power to run the nation the way they wanted.

troubadours: people who sing while strolling around an area.

Religion and Power

oday, we may view Queen Isabella with both admiration and frustration. While she was a champion for women's rights, she was at the same time opposed to any freedom of religion. A deeply devout and sincere Christian, she and Ferdinand became known as "Les Rois Catholiques," which means, "The Catholic Royalty."

Nowadays, we talk about the separation of church and state—the idea that religious leaders should not run governments. In the Middle Ages, however, people assumed religious leaders would control political affairs. At that time, religious believers—both Christian and Muslim—assumed that kings and queens should make laws and go to war to defend their faith. Wealthy nobles bought, fought, and sometimes assassinated their way into church leadership so they could gain power. At the time of Isabella and Ferdinand, Spanish Catholics were resentful toward Muslims, who had taken over their kingdoms centuries earlier. Prejudice and misunderstanding also colored their thinking about Jews.

Just a few years after they became King and Queen, Ferdinand and Isabella asked the Pope for permission to create a new government office in Spain—the Inquisition. It was the job of the Inquisition to find and punish heretics—people who did not follow the beliefs of the Catholic Church. Since Muslims had ruled most of Spain for centuries, thousands of them were still living there. There were also more than 170,000 Jews. Under the Inquisition, Jews and Muslims had three choices—convert to Christianity, leave Spain, or be tortured to death.

Enormous crowds rushed to the ports of Spain, fleeing for their lives. Not all escaped. More than 30,000 Jews, Muslims, and other "heretics" were tortured and killed by the Spanish Inquisition. Keep this in mind as we go further in this book and learn about the horrible ways Native people were treated by Spanish conquerors in the Americas. If they rejected Christianity, Indians were treated as the "heretics" were in Spain.

 n 1492, three things happened that were tremendously helpful for Spain. These three events also shaped the future history of the Americas. Granada fell, a new Pope was elected, and Ferdinand and Isabella gambled on a very unlikely chance, which proved to be history's luckiest dare.

The Fall of Granada

 or hundreds of years, Christian knights in the Iberian Peninsula had been fighting Muslims, whom they called the Moors, who had conquered these lands in the year 711.

The Renaissance

he Golden Age of Spain is also the time in history known as the Renaissance—or "rebirth" of European culture. Scholars began to rediscover the achievements in art and science made by the Greeks and Romans in ancient times. This influenced great artists like Michelangelo and Botticelli, architects like Bernini who built the Vatican, and inventors like Leonardo da Vinci. New discoveries in world travel, happening at the same time as these great artistic advances, made it an exciting time indeed.

The Christians had learned much from their Arab conquerors. The Moors introduced a much greater variety of healthy foods to eat, taught the Christians more sophisticated techniques of architecture, and shared principles of advanced mathematics and science. Nonetheless, the two faiths were continually at odds. The Crusades—wars fought between Christians and Muslims for control of Jerusalem—added to the tension.

Slowly, the knights of Castile and Aragon pushed Islam southward. The battles they fought were called the Reconquista—the reconquest of their old lands. Finally, only Granada remained. As long as the Christian kingdoms were divided and fought each other, they could not defeat this Muslim stronghold.

When Isabella and Ferdinand united their two kingdoms, however, the new nation of Spain had enough military power to defeat Granada. There was tremendous rejoicing among the Christians when this last Moorish outpost was conquered.

The Reconquista produced a special breed of men—conquistadors, soldiers who fought for their religion and to gain lands for Spain. These men would lead the invasion of the Americas.

A New Pope

n the same year that Granada fell, the Catholic Church came under a new leader. The man who was declared Pope in 1492 was born with the name Rodrigo Borgia. A wealthy Spaniard, he bought votes to become the supreme head of the Church. When he became Pope, he took the name Alexander VI. He had no objection to playing favorites—he gave every advantage he could to Isabella and Ferdinand, rulers of his native land. When an explorer flying the Spanish flag discovered a vast new continent, this Pope was pleased to declare all those lands the property of Spain—requiring the Natives to become Christians.

An Adventuresome Sailor

he third important thing that happened in 1492 involved a sailor who had for years been seeking sponsors for an unlikely ocean voyage. He was born in Genoa, Italy, with the name Cristoforo Colombo. After moving to Spain he changed his name to sound more Spanish—Cristóbal Colón. In the English-speaking world, he is known as Christopher Columbus.

Columbus was a highly skilled ship's captain and a deeply religious man. A mixture of ideas—which he got from the Bible, astrology, and what he claimed was the voice of God—told him he would fulfill a unique purpose in history.

Reformation

n 1517, a German monk named Martin Luther began to voice disagreements he had with the Pope. This led to the splitting of the Catholic Church. Those who left the church were known as Protestants, or Reformers—hence, this time in history is also known as the Reformation.

Spanish Catholic leaders in the 1500s looked at the world as a four-way religious competition. They were determined to defeat Muslims, Jews, and Protestants whatever way they could. This sense of religious competition influenced the conquest of the Americas in two ways. Spain wanted to claim all the land it could for the Catholic Church, and the religious wars in Europe required gold and silver from the New World to supply armies back in Spain.

Under Ferdinand and Isabella, the Catholic faith had triumphed in Spain. Why should they not go all the way, and win back the Holy Land from Islam? If they did so, Jesus would return to judge the world and reward his servants. A crusade to liberate the Holy Land would take great wealth to accomplish—much gold would be needed to sup-

What's in a Name?

Do you believe your name determines what will happen in your life? Christopher Columbus believed his name gave him clues to his destiny. Saint Christopher is the patron saint of travelers—appropriate for a man who wanted to make a dangerous journey across the ocean. Also, Christopher literally means "Christ bearer." Columbus believed it was his destiny to bring knowledge of Christ to the people of the Indies.

port the conquering army. Gold was hard to come by in 1492, as the Muslims had cut off trade routes to Africa and Asia. Columbus had a plan to get that gold. He would sail across the Atlantic Ocean to Asia. Queen Isabella and King Ferdinand decided to take a chance and give him three ships for his voyage.

There is an old myth that people believed the world was flat, so they feared Columbus might sail right off the edge. In fact, all educated people in 1492 knew the world was a globe. It wasn't the shape of the world that caused folks to laugh at Columbus—it was the size. Columbus had calculated how far he would have to sail to reach Asia. He figured half the distance everyone else guessed. He was a good sailor but a poor mathematician. Fortunately for Columbus—and for Ferdinand and Isabella who paid for his journey—there was a whole New World where he was headed.

Habla Español

el rey (ail ray): the king

la reina (lah ray-eena): the queen

iglesia (ee-glace-ee-ah): church

Keeping Up with the Neighbors

he Kingdom of Portugal, which stretches across the Atlantic Coast of the Iberian Peninsula, was world famous for sea travel in the time of Ferdinand and Isabella. Under Prince Henry, known as "the navigator," Portuguese sailors discovered and mapped much of the world we know today. They opened seaways to the coasts of Africa and, unfortunately, began the slave trade. The Portuguese explorer Vasco da Gama succeeded in doing exactly what Columbus hoped to do—he found an ocean route to India that gave Portugal a valuable trade route for spices.

Superior technology helped the Portuguese make these trips. By combining Arab and European styles, they were able to manufacture the world's best ships. Magnetic compasses, detailed ocean charts, and other new inventions made navigation across the open ocean possible.

Odd as it may seem, the Portuguese's great knowledge of the ocean caused them to miss history's greatest opportunity. Columbus asked repeatedly for Portugal to give him ships for his voyage across the Atlantic. The King assigned a group of scientists to study Columbus's claims. They decided—rightly—that he would never reach Asia heading in that direction.

Since Portugal would not help him, Columbus took his ideas to Spain. Hoping for a discovery that would help them keep up with their high-achieving neighbors, Ferdinand and Isabella decided to give Columbus a chance.

3

First Contact

*An age will come after many years
when the Ocean will loose the chains of
things, and a huge land lie revealed.*
—Seneca, ancient Greek poet

*This prophecy was fulfilled by my father, the Admiral, in
the year 1492.*
—Ferdinand Columbus, the son of Christopher

"Tierra! Tierra!" yelled Martin Alonso Pinzón from the *poop deck* of the *Pinta*. "Land! Land! I claim the reward!" Sailors rushed to side-rails and scrambled up the ratlines, all with eyes straining forward to see for themselves. As the coastline became visible, cheers burst from weary throats. None of the crew realized, on that day, the full importance of what was taking place. In the future, Europeans would think of this first contact with a New World across the Atlantic as the turning point of their history.

For Admiral Christopher Columbus, it was the blessed *confirmation* of everything he had staked his life on for the past nine years. In 1483, living in Lisbon, Portugal, Columbus had come to firmly believe that China and India could be reached by sailing due west across the Atlantic. Europeans had recently rediscovered ancient Greek and Roman literature, and Columbus noticed, "Aristotle says between the end of Spain and the beginning of India is a small sea navigable in a few days." He was convinced God had chosen him to sail this way and open up a glorious new trade route for the Catholic nations.

After a few wasted years trying to convince the Portuguese royalty to give him a ship for the journey, Columbus took his *radical* ideas to Spain. There, he spent six more miserable years, living in dire poverty, attempting to sell his idea to Ferdinand and Isabella. Columbus's time in Spain has been described as "a terrible, continuous, painful, complex battle." He faced humiliating ridicule and repeated refusals at the Spanish court.

In January 1492, he held a final meeting with Queen Isabella. He requested ships, the title of admiral, the right to be governor of lands he discovered, and 10 percent of the profits from the Orient after he established trade there. "That's my final offer, your majesty—you may take it or leave it."

Isabella said no.

Columbus with Ferdinand and Isabella

Columbus went home, packed his mule, and with his two sons and mistress started on his way to France where perhaps King Charles would listen. But before he got to the Spanish border, a messenger stopped him—the queen had changed her mind! He would have three ships and everything else he had asked for.

At first, the journey westward went smoothly. Trade winds pushed the little fleet quickly across the ocean. They saw strange sights. *Phosphorous* sea creatures lit up the *wake* of the three ships at night. They crossed the Sargasso Sea, covered with floating vegetation. Their compass started going haywire as they crossed over magnetic fields. Columbus knew his men would be nervous sailing too far into the unknown. Each day, he told them how far they had come—but he reported far less than the actual distance traveled. The real distances were in a private journal locked tight in his cabin.

After three weeks, the crew threatened to *mutiny*. Even according to the phony reports he gave them, they were much farther from land than any sailors had ever gone. They were past the point where their supplies would allow them to return. The crew was Spanish, and Columbus was an Italian, so they looked down on him as a foreigner. With

Christopher Columbus

their hands on the hilts of their swords, the crew demanded he turn the ship around—or else!

Columbus was undaunted. "I have come this far to reach the Indies, and I must continue westward until we reach them, with the help of our Lord." He argued for a compromise—three more days and he would head back. By the third day, the crew had seen branches with leaves floating in the water. It was obvious to all that Columbus's mad fantasy would be realized—land was near.

Imagine how different history would be if Christopher Columbus had been less determined—and less persuasive.

The Arawak

The Arawak

unters of the Taino branch of Arawak people stood quietly on the beach, ready to flee or fight if need be. They kept their eyes on the strangers, noting their every move. Runners had sped inland and word was spreading throughout the island of Guanahaní (since Columbus's landing, known as San Salvador, in the Bahamas). Three enormous canoes with white wings had suddenly appeared out in the ocean. Now, men were coming ashore in a smaller canoe. These men were covered in bright clothes from head to foot; some of them were dressed in shiny metal. They were like no tribe anyone in the Taino band had ever seen or heard of. Who were these men? Did they mean good or ill?

The Arawak had just discovered Europeans. They watched as the little boat beached. A tall man with red hair and a crimson cape on his shoulders, obviously the leader, stepped onto the beach holding a banner. He put it in the ground and sank down to his knees, looking up at the sky and speaking out loud. He was apparently working magic or speaking to the spirits. As more Arawak stepped out of the brush to see this strange sight, the leader of the strangers turned to address them. He made impressive gestures and spoke what they assumed were medicine words. If only the Arawak could have understood Spanish! They would have shuddered—or become enraged—if they had heard Christopher Columbus renaming their island with the name of his God, then declaring all of them subject to King Ferdinand and Queen Isabella.

friar: *a man who belongs to any of several Roman Catholic religious orders.*

Columbus himself tells what happened next:

In order that they would be friendly to us—because I recognized they were people who would be better freed from error and converted to our holy faith by love than by force—to some I gave red caps, and glass beads which they put on their chests, and many other things of small value, in which they took so much pleasure and became so much our friends that it was a marvel.

The Arawaks in turn presented parrots, cotton thread, and other items to the strangers.

This first contact between people from two different hemispheres appeared civil enough. Each side was delighted with what the others presented. The sailors were a bit surprised by the nudity of the Natives—this wasn't how they expected people from Asia to dress. They were, at the same time, greatly pleased to see gold jewelry glistening against the Natives' dark skin.

Later, Columbus recorded his true thoughts in his private journal. The natives would "become Christians very easily, for it seems they have no religion." He also noted they would "make good and intelligent slaves." He decided to take some of them back to Spain as captives.

From the beginning, Europeans saw Native Americans as the fulfillment for their selfish wishes. Columbus regarded them as childlike, innocent people. He assumed they would willingly serve Spanish masters. He named them Indians, since he wrongly believed he was in the outer reaches of India. A mistake—but the word has stuck. To this day, Native people of the Americas are called "Indians" in the English-speaking world, or "Indios" in Spanish. Less than a century after Columbus, a Spanish *friar* noted "the natives do not like to be called 'Indians'

A Whole List of "Firsts"

Columbus and his crew were the first Europeans to experience a number of things we take for granted today.

• The Indians of Hispaniola slept in hammocks—which sailors and others soon discovered were wonderful for sleeping on ships—or for relaxing in the yard.

• The Indians gave Columbus's men potatoes and yams. Potatoes would help portions of Europe to survive through famines in later years.

• The Indians also introduced their European visitors to smoking leaves—tobacco. They informed the Spaniards that the substance was pleasurable but also addictive— as all too many people during the last five centuries have found out for themselves.

Reconstruction of the Nina, *the* Pinta, *and the* Santa Maria

since that is not what they call themselves." Today, many Native people still prefer to identify themselves by the name of their tribe, Tarahumara, Cherokee, Zuni, and so on.

Gold, God, and Slaves

s soon as they could communicate, the Spaniards asked where the Indians got their gold. Gestures were made to communicate, "The next island." It was an answer that Columbus's men would hear again and again—and they kept sailing after the *elusive* treasure. They navigated more of the Bahamas, then sailed on to Cuba, and then on again to the island of Hispaniola.

On Hispaniola, tragedy struck on Christmas Day. The *Santa Maria* ran onto a submerged coral reef and tore her bottom out. The *Pinta* had abandoned the other two ships, as its captain wanted to find gold for himself. So Columbus had crewmen from two ships, with only one to carry them. He prayed and sought some divine explanation for this sour turn of events.

He soon got his answer—it was God's will for them to form a colony here! So Columbus set about building a simple fort. When the *Pinta* reappeared, Columbus left one ship's crew on Hispaniola, promising to return soon.

Returning to Spain, Columbus was cheered as a hero. The enslaved Indians, tropical birds, and—especially—the gold jewelry that he brought from "the Indies" were a big hit. No one asked the Indians what they thought of being kidnapped and brought overseas as exhibits. Columbus was given the title, "Don Cristóbal Colón, Admiral of the Ocean Sea, Viceroy and Governor of the Islands he has discovered in the Indies."

elusive: hard to achieve or get.

Columbus's Return

fter years of people making fun of his ideas, Columbus had the last laugh and he enjoyed rubbing it in all he could.

Unknowingly, the ships' crews also brought an invisible passenger back to Spain—syphilis. Native Americans had, over the centuries, built up a tolerance to the sexually transmitted disease. It is not clear who was having sex with whom, but shortly after the *Niña* and *Pinta* returned to the Old World, syphilis spread as a terrible plague from the Spanish port towns into the rest of Europe. But the effect of this disease on Europe was small compared to what European germs would eventually do to Native populations in the Western Hemisphere.

First Conflict

he newly proclaimed "Viceroy and Governor of the Islands he has discovered" was anxious to return to his lands, and was soon under way with a larger fleet of ships. On returning to Hispaniola, he sadly realized it wasn't the paradise he had hoped for. Indians had wiped out the little colony he left there. Through a Native translator, Columbus got the sad story. After their ships left, the Spaniards had gotten about the business of exploiting the Indians. They marched around the island, raped women, and forced the Natives to give them gold. The Indians went to war to free themselves from this tyranny. It was a profound disappointment to the Spanish that these people they had *stereotyped* as childlike would actually rather fight than be enslaved, robbed, and molested.

Columbus continued to sail around the Caribbean searching for the cities, gold, and spices he expected to find in the Orient. He was frustrated to find nothing like them. Although he proposed to the crown that a fair profit could be made selling Indians for slaves, the first discoveries in the West Indies weren't as profitable as had been hoped. Columbus was a poor governor, and things went so badly under his leadership that he was sent back to Spain in chains after his fourth trip. Despite his amazing achievements, Christopher Columbus died a broken man.

Map of Spain's colonies

An Age of Exploration—and Exploitation

o the end of his life, Columbus believed he had reached Asia. He was sure that further exploration would prove him right. It took a number of years for Spanish mapmakers to realize what had actually happened. As more and more ships went back and forth across the Atlantic, maps began to be drawn. Europeans gradually realized this was not Asia, but—even more magnificent—a vast pair of continents they had never known before. There were advanced cultures with enormous cities filled with gold, even more impressive than the Oriental capitals they had origi- nally hoped to find. Columbus's discovery was greater than he could ever have dreamed.

Bartoleme de las Casas

The Spanish regarded this New World as theirs by right of discovery, and the Pope quickly confirmed this. As incredible as it is to us today, they never considered the fact that these continents were already filled with people who should have been respected as the owners of their own lands. Some Spaniards—like the priest Bartoleme de las Casas—tried to prevent the slaughter of Indians, but others questioned whether people of other races were even human.

For many Europeans and their descendants, Christopher Columbus continues to be a larger-than-life hero. Francisco López de Gómara spoke for many when he declared in 1552 that Columbus's discovery was "the greatest event since the creation of the world" except for the birth of Christ. We can still admire Columbus's seamanship and courage even as we are saddened by the way that he treated Native Americans.

For the Native Americans, contact with Europe was the beginning of a battle for cultural survival that continues. Historians have studied the horrific number of Native American deaths following contact with Europe. They conclude that it may be history's worst case of *genocide*. No one knows for sure how many Native people died following Columbus's voyage, but an average estimate is around 40 million in the first hundred years. Although many were murdered by the European invaders, many more died from diseases to which they had no immunity.

Caucasians had been in the Western Hemisphere before Columbus—the Vikings landed on the East Coast, and Irish monks may have visited the Americas. Yet their visits were just blips on the radar screen of history. After Columbus, for better or worse, the fates of Europe and the Americas were bound together. Whether you admire him or hate him, you have to admit: Columbus forever changed the world.

Amerigo Vespucci Wins "Name That Continent"

 olumbus died believing the lands he had come to were part of Asia. Another explorer, Amerigo Vespucci, is supposed to have sailed westward shortly after Columbus. Historians have doubts about his claims. Vespucci, unlike Columbus, realized these newly discovered lands were not Asia but, as he put it, "a New World." As a consequence, mapmakers named the continents America—after Amerigo. Columbus certainly deserved far more than Amerigo to have these continents named after him; but history is often unfair.

 **Habla Español**

barco (bark-oh): ship

marinero (mah-ree-nare-oh): sailor

mar (mahr): ocean

47

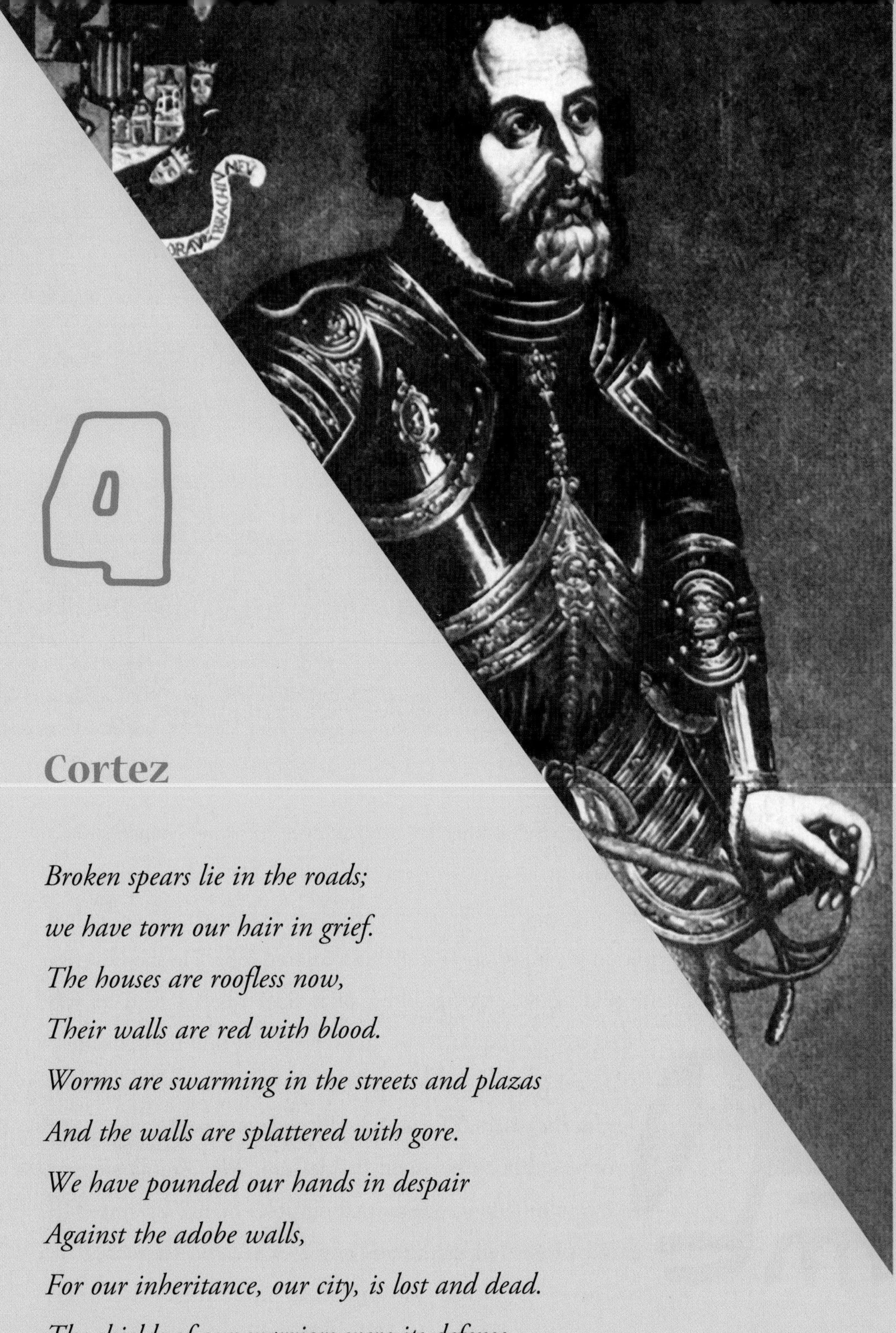

Cortez

Broken spears lie in the roads;

we have torn our hair in grief.

The houses are roofless now,

Their walls are red with blood.

Worms are swarming in the streets and plazas

And the walls are splattered with gore.

We have pounded our hands in despair

Against the adobe walls,

For our inheritance, our city, is lost and dead.

The shields of our warriors were its defense

But they could not save it.

—ancient Mexican poem, mourning the fall of Tenochtitlan

Map of the city of Tenochtitlan

"O gods, why has this day been allowed to come?" Moctezuma's face was lined with worry as he prayed. He had ordered sacrifices and said farewell to his wives and children. Then he had put on his finest, most brilliantly colored robe. He shod his feet in gold sandals. A headdress of radiant quetzal feathers was placed upon his head. Now, he stepped out into the sunshine.

Two thousand nobles stood in formation, ready to march from the palace. Moctezuma's brother and nephew, rulers of other great cities, stood beside him. Moctezuma stepped into a mobile throne carried on poles by his servants. The grand procession, as fine as any ever seen in Tenochtitlan, headed slowly across the bridge to meet these mysterious strangers of whom they had heard so much.

Across the bridge, the strangers came to meet them. They rode beasts that looked like enormous deer, which pranced and snorted with frightening sounds. The men were dressed in suits

No Turning Back

hortly after Cortez's fleet landed on the Mexican coast in 1519, there were some members of the expedition who grumbled about the wisdom of heading into the heart of the Aztec Empire. Fearing his men might try and sail back to Cuba, Cortez ordered the ships to be sailed up onto the beach and torn apart so their wood and metal could be recycled for other purposes. As Cortez later recalled, "then they [his company] had nothing to rely on, apart from their own hands. . . . They would conquer and win the land or die in the attempt."

of glittering metal. Their swords, helmets, and shields were made of the same substance, and some of the beasts wore metal covers as well. On the tops of their long spears, the strangers' banners flapped in the wind. Behind the riders came footmen, pale-faced like the others. Behind them walked thousands of Tlaxcalla warriors, longtime enemies of the Mexica.

As the strangers approached the bridge, hundreds of canoes crowded the waterways. All the citizens of Tenochtitlan were eager for a glimpse of these strange creatures. Mexica scouts had been bringing news of these newcomers for more than a year. The strangers first arrived at the coast in enormous canoes, which they sank as soon as they had disem-

Aztec drawing

barked. The white men had walked further and further inland, fighting and defeating the other tribes with strange magical logs that thundered and threw fiery death, or else entering into alliances with the Mexica's enemies along the way. Now, they had arrived at the center of the world.

The two thousand nobles whom Moctezuma had sent ahead approached the strangers two at a time, bowing with their faces to the ground. This took several hours. Finally, the Huey Tlatoani himself approached the newcomers.

As the two parties came face to face, Moctezuma stepped down from his mobile throne and walked forward calmly, apparently unafraid. The leader of the strangers dismounted and walked toward him. He reached out a hand, and firmly grasped the hand of the Tlatoani. Under normal circumstances, he would have been killed. None dared touch the leader of the Mexica without his bidding. But these were no ordinary visitors. Moctezuma was uncertain whether they were mortal like him or visitors from the spirit world.

This was the year Cane 1 on the Mexica calendar (A.D. 1519 for the Europeans), and ancient prophecies predicted the return of Quetzalcoatl—the white god—in this year. Could this being who stood before Moctezuma, bearded and dressed in shiny cloth and metal, be the Second Coming of Quetzalcoatl?

Moctezuma would have been less impressed if he could have known Hernando Cortez the way his fellow Spaniards knew him. His father had been a soldier, proven in the battles of the Reconquista. As a young man, Cortez sailed to Cuba, where he was put in charge of a *hacienda* (ranch). There, he earned a reputation for two things—seducing women and gambling. Oddly, these two dishonorable traits represented talents that would enable him to conquer a great empire. Women weren't the only ones charmed—and fooled—by

Cortez building boats with the help of Natives

Cortez. He had an amazing knack for convincing people to believe in him and do whatever he wanted. This enabled him to win the loyalty of fellow conquistadors, who would follow him to the ends of the earth if need be.

He was also able to win the trust of Indians he met on the way to Tenochtitlan. These tribes resented the taxes and sacrificial offerings they made to the Mexica Empire. The chiefs of these tribes believed Cortez's promises of reward for helping him defeat the Mexicas. Unfortunately, Cortez could be a great liar, and they would in turn become slaves and victims of the Spanish when Cortez was done with them.

His success at gambling also represented a strength. In war and diplomacy, he had amazing timing. He knew the instant to attack, the right occasion to flatter, and the

The site of Tenochtitlan

moment when he needed to turn on a previous *ally*. In Cuba, he had earned the governor's approval for an expedition to claim Mexico for Castile. Then, the governor realized that Cortez was doing things differently than he had been told to do them. Against orders, Cortez went ahead and sailed with his ships and men. As far as his own countrymen were concerned, he was a *renegade* on this expedition. Cortez was a villain, even according to some of his fellow Castilians—but a brilliant one.

At last, Moctezuma spoke to the conquistador. "O Lord, you have suffered fatigue and endured weariness. You have now arrived on earth. You have come to govern Tenochtitlan; you have come to sit upon the throne, which I have guarded for you until today. My ancestors also waited for your return, and now you have come to sit upon your throne. All is fulfilled. Rest yourself, stay in your palace."

Cortez, obviously pleased, replied that he came in the name of the King and Queen of Spain, who were rightful rulers of this land. He came to gain Moctezuma's obedience to them and also to the True God whom they served. This was the first great misunderstanding between them—the Huey Tlatoani believed he was speaking to one of the gods, and Cortez happily assumed he was receiving submission to the Spanish crown.

Moctezuma presented to Cortez a necklace of pure gold. The conquistador asked if there was much more gold like this in the Mexica Empire. Moctezuma unwisely replied that yes, there was much more gold—and Cortez said he was pleased, "For my men have a sickness, which can only be cured by gold."

Of course, Moctezuma and Cortez could not understand each other's words without translation. That was the job of the tall, fine-featured Indian woman who stood at Cortez's side throughout his conquest of Mexico. In every picture of the Conquistador Captain, she is beside him, her long black hair flowing down to her waist. Europeans noted, "She was beautiful as a goddess." The Mexica said, "It was shocking to see a woman of our race leading the Spaniards to Mexico." Her name was Malinche.

Malinche was an astonishment and an *enigma* to Indians and Spaniards alike—both then and now. Cortez himself wrote, "After God, we owe this conquest of Mexico to Doña Marina" (her Spanish name).

Malinche was born to a noble Mexica family. When her father died, her mother remarried and sold her daughter as a slave to the Tabasco tribe. The Tabascos were one of the tribes conquered and ruled by the Mexica. When Cortez arrived, the Tabasco gave Malinche to the conquistador as a gift. She quickly gained favor with Cortez as translator, advisor, and

ally: *someone who joins another in support of a mutual goal.*

renegade: *someone who voluntarily lives outside what is considered normal for a particular group.*

enigma: *a mystery.*

lover. Those who watched this Indian woman translate for Cortez were sometimes unsure whether she rendered word for word, or if her own subtle ideas were influencing the course of events. She bore him a son, who has been referred to as "the first Mexican" (in other words, the first child born of a union between a Spaniard and Mexica Indian). Cortez was devoted to Malinche, even though he slept with many other women. He is said to have strangled his Spanish wife, but he apparently treated Malinche with respect.

To this day, Malinche is a source of fascination and controversy. A traitor to Mexico is called a *malinchista*, yet historians claim she repeatedly used her influence with Cortez to prevent him from killing her fellow Indians. She is portrayed as a prostitute—and as a virtuous Christian. She is seen as a puppet for the Spanish, but also as a strong, independent woman—the first Latina *feminist*. We will never really know what motivated her, but one thing is certain—she was one of the most influential people in the entire history of Mexico.

Aztec drawing

Soon after the grand entrance of Spanish soldiers into Tenochtitlan, events began that would lead to the Aztecs' demise. The Spaniards were in awe of this great city, which was larger, more beautiful, and cleaner than any city in Castile. They knew they were outnumbered a hundred to one by Mexica warriors. Yet, in their arrogance, the Europeans were certain the Aztec Empire would soon be theirs. The Castilian troops took Moctezuma hostage in his own palace. They made him give orders for them—requesting gold, women, and information. For several months, the Huey Tlatoani served as a puppet for the Castilians.

Then Cortez got alarming news. A Spanish army, twice the size of his own, was marching inland. They had been sent from Cuba to arrest Cortez and bring him back. Taking half his soldiers, Cortez marched into the jungle where he ambushed the forces from Cuba, wounding their commander. Using his gift for charm, Cortez talked the rest of the Cuban army into joining him.

Arriving back at Tenochtitlan with his now enlarged army, Cortez discovered things had gone awry in his absence. The commander left in charge, Pedro de Alvarado, had ordered his men to attack the Mexica while they were enjoying a religious festival.

Men, women, and children, dressed in their finest outfits—clothing adorned with macaw feathers, specially woven cloaks, turquoise bracelets, and gold lip plugs—had gathered for the festival of Huitzilopochtli. They sang and danced to the beat of hollow drums. Suddenly, thunderous explosions rang out—shots from Spanish muskets. Conquistadors covered in steel armor strode into the square, slashing their swords through skin and bone of the unarmed Indian dancers. They fired, reloaded, thrust, and hacked until the temple grounds were covered with disfigured corpses.

Cortez was upset when he returned and heard about the massacre. It wasn't that he regretted the taking of lives—but Cortez realized the massacre was a strategic blunder. The Castilians were holed up in Moctezuma's palace, which was in the center of an island. The mainland could only be reached by crossing narrow bridges. They had trapped themselves.

Once again, Moctezuma was paraded before his subjects with orders from the Spanish. This time, the Aztecs knew they were being duped. A hail of deadly darts greeted Moctezuma and his Spanish captors. The Huey Tlatoani fell dead. The Castilians would have to find another way out of the capital.

feminist: someone who believes that women should have equal rights with men.

Aztec painting of the founding of Tenochtitlan

On the night of July 1, in a light rain, Cortez's army attempted to sneak out of the palace. A long procession of Spanish soldiers, the women they had acquired, and their Tlaxcalla allies silently headed across the westward bridge. The Castilians were weighed down with gold they had taken. Their horses' hooves were wrapped in cloth to quiet them, and the entire company moved as silently as they could.

They were halfway across the bridge, and beginning to think they would escape safely, when a voice cried out. Within minutes, the dark sky was filled with a hail of arrows and darts. Canoes swarmed all around the bridge. The Mexica relentlessly shot arrows and darts into the mass of Spanish and Tlaxcalla soldiers. Visibility was limited in the dark, and the Castilians were pressed tightly together. It was hard to load and fire their muskets and crossbows. Screams, curses, and the neighing of panicked horses echoed across the waterway. Obsidian-tipped darts came smashing through *chain mail*, as the Spaniards learned a horrible lesson in the efficiency of Aztec weapons.

With the heavy gold affecting their ability to escape, the Europeans faced a classic dilemma—would they abandon their money to save their lives? Desperate, Castilian sol-

An Ancient Weapon and a New Sport

esides bows and arrows, Aztec warriors used a spear-throwing device called the atlatl. This weapon had been used for more than 10,000 years throughout the Americas. It consists of a flexible piece of wood, approximately two feet long, with a hook on the far end. A spear or large dart fits into this hook. With an atlatl, darts can be thrown much harder and further than with the unaided arm. Tipped with razor-sharp obsidian blades, Aztec atlatl darts were lethal indeed.

Nowadays, hobby enthusiasts in the United States, Mexico, and Europe enjoy the atlatl. An organization called the World Atlatl Association is dedicated to promoting the sport. Contests are held for accuracy and distance throws. A small number of sportsmen also use the primitive weapon for hunting and fishing.

diers climbed over the bodies of their wounded comrades and pushed Tlaxcalla allies off the bridge to hasten their flight.

When the horror of that night had ended, more than six hundred Spanish and a thousand Tlaxcalla were dead. Another

chain mail: *a knight's armor, made of interlinked rings of metal.*

270 Spaniards remained trapped in the palace. They were later sacrificed to Huitzilopochtli, without the benefit of anesthetic drugs that were ordinarily given to victims. Whenever they recalled this night, the Spanish called it *Noche Triste*, which means "night of grief."

With most of his army destroyed, vastly outnumbered, and in the midst of a hostile empire, any other leader would have run for home and safety. Not Cortez. As the survivors regrouped on the mainland, the conquistador captain was far from daunted. He asked if Martin Lopez, the ship builder, had survived.

"*Sí, Capitán*, he is injured but he will live."

"Good!" exclaimed Cortez, "We lack nothing." Incredibly, after a night of awful defeat, he was already strategizing the next step in his conquest.

Through the summer of 1520, the Spanish prepared to attack Tenochtitlan. Camping with his forces in Tlaxcalla, Cortez convinced more Indians to join with them, and by the winter, he had gathered an alliance of more than 200,000 Indians prepared to war against the Mexica.

The Aztec god of medicine

After the disaster fleeing the capital, Cortez realized a naval force was necessary to take the city. He put his army to work constructing boats in prefabricated sections, which could be taken to the lake and quickly put together for the assault.

In the meantime, another enemy, even deadlier than the Spaniards, had invaded the Aztec capital. Smallpox swept through Tenochtitlan, and for seventy days, men and women, young and old, from the palace to the huts of commoners, cried out in agony. Countless Mexica died. The plague was so severe that normal social structures broke down. One of the Aztecs later recalled,

An Invisible Killer

ou may think that guns and swords were responsible for the European conquest of the Americas—but really an invisible killer wiped out far more Native people than did the Europeans' superior weapons. In the centuries after Columbus landed in the New World in 1492, more native North Americans died each year from infectious diseases brought by the European settlers than were born. Germs were the Indians' worst enemy.

Many types of diseases were brought into the Americas; the main ones were smallpox, measles, influenza, and typhus, as well as whooping cough, the mumps, and diphtheria. When a person is exposed to the germs that cause these illnesses, he will usually become sick. If he does not die, however, his body will have created antibodies to protect him from becoming infected again by the same germs. In other words, he will have immunity to that particular germ.

Many types of infectious diseases are carried by animals and passed along to humans. Europeans lived close to various types of domestic animals, and so they had plenty of opportunities to come in contact with many types of infectious disease and develop immunities. Each generation had also developed genetic material that made people more resistant to disease. (Through natural selection, people who have acquired disease-resistant genes are more likely to survive.)

In the Americas, however, there were only a few domesticated animals, which did not carry harmful germs, so the transference of disease from animals to humans was unlikely. In fact, the Americas were considered virtually disease-free. Since North and South America had no exposure to European diseases, severe outbreaks of disease were destined to occur once the newcomers arrived. We will probably never know how many people died as a result of the Europeans' arrival in the Americas.

"Many died from hunger for they had no one to look after them." As the plague subsided, the Mexica appointed a new leader, Cuauhtemoc. He was young, brave, and skilled in battle—but his army was greatly reduced by the smallpox.

In December of 1520, the small Spanish army and their legions of Indian comrades marched on Tenochtitlan. Eight thousand Indian workers carried forty large boats in sections over the hills to the lakeside. The boats were assembled, and Cortez's troops attacked from the south.

It was a desperate, hard-fought battle. The Mexica knew their entire way of life was at stake, and they were determined to battle furiously for every street. House to house, step by step, the battle raged for eighty days. Women fought alongside the men, every Mexica determined to give all for the homeland. Finally, when only a little corner of the island remained, Cuauhtemoc and his captains gathered to discuss their final step. Clearly, defeat was inevitable, and an omen in the sky, perhaps a comet or large meteor, convinced the Huey Tlatoani to surrender.

According to Alva Ixtililxochitl, the Aztec historian who wrote about it eighty years later:

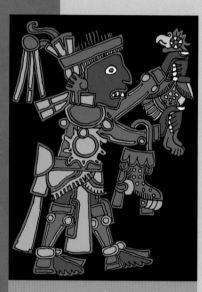

Aztec drawing

> On the day that Tenochtitlan was taken, the Spaniards committed some of the most brutal acts ever inflicted upon the unfortunate people of this land. The cries of the helpless women and children were heart-rending. The Tlaxcalans and other enemies of the Aztecs revenged themselves pitilessly for old offences and robbed them of everything they had. . . . Warriors gathered on the rooftops and stared at the ruins of their city in a dazed silence, and the women and children and old men were all weeping.

Rebirth of Mexico City

hen the conquistadors first walked into Tenochtitlan, they were amazed by the city. It was as large and beautiful as any metropolis they had ever seen. During the horrific fighting of the conquest, the city was largely reduced to rubble. Though Tenochtitlan had ended, a new city, named Mexico City after the Mexica people, arose in its place. Many of the stones from the old city were reused for churches, government buildings, and fortifications of the new Spanish capital of Mexico. Today, with 20 million inhabitants, Mexico City is again one of the greatest cities in the world.

 Habla Español

guerra (gare-ah): war

vida (vee-dah): life

muerta (mware-tah): death

5

Conquistadors

Even if all the snow in the Andes turned to gold,
still they [the Spanish] would not be satisfied.
—Inca Manco

"Comrades and friends, on that side lies the part which represents death, hardship, hunger, nakedness and abandonment; this side here represents comfort. Here you return to Panama—to be poor! There you may go on to Peru—to be rich. You choose which best fits you as brave Spaniards."

Francisco Pizarro said these words after drawing a line in the sand with his sword. It was August of 1527, and the place was Isla de Gallo, an uninhabited island just off the shore of Colombia. Pizarro was speaking to eighty men facing one of the most important choices they would ever make.

A Difficult Choice

hey had followed him thus far attempting to reach a fabled Indian kingdom in Peru, one with fabulous riches. So far, the expedition had not gone well. They were eating snakes and clams, and some had died from hunger or illness. There were those among the expedition who said Pizarro was a lunatic, who would cause them all to die before they reached Peru. Now, a ship had come to take those who wished back to Panama. Pizarro drew his line in the sand to see how many would choose to follow him on to Peru.

Only thirteen chose to do so. The others sailed away, leaving the explorers stranded on a deserted island. For another seven months, they struggled to survive. Yet, as Pizarro promised, riches and fame eventually became theirs.

Pizarro

Pizarro

ho was this man, Francisco Pizarro? He was fifty years old at the time of the incident just described. In his younger years, he had served as a soldier in Spain, then went to Panama where he gained wealth as part owner of a gold mine.

Pizarro was ruthless. He personally tortured Native leaders to make them tell where gold could be found. One man who knew him said, "Committing cruelties against the Indians was a habit Pizarro knew by heart."

When a ship arrived to take Pizarro and his hungry companions back to Panama, Pizarro insisted they sail south to Peru. They did so, and reached the Native town of Tumbes. There, the Spaniards saw Indians—the Incas—who impressed them with their "rational" civilization, handsome appearance, and—most important—abundance of gold. Through gestures and translation, Pizarro informed the Native governor that he had come to claim the land for the king of Spain who lived across the ocean. The Inca leader found this speech rather humorous. He would have been less amused if he could have foreseen the invasion that would follow.

Francisco Pizarro and his companions returned to Panama and reported what they had seen. His brothers, Hernando, Juan, and Gonzalo, joined him. Together they began one of the richest and most powerful family enterprises in history. The brothers were given ships and soldiers and sent southward in

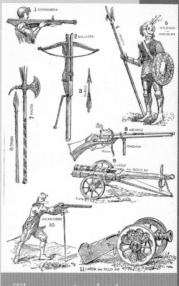

The conquistadors' weapons

67

The Inca's ancient city of Machu Picchu now lies in ruins.

December of 1530 to conquer the Inca Empire. Those men who had stood by Francisco Pizarro when he drew his line in the sand went with him on this expedition.

A Mighty Empire

he Native empire in Peru was indeed a rich prize. Although the Inca did not know the Aztecs, their empire was just as powerful. They ruled 25,000 square miles (65,000 square kilometers) that covered parts of Colombia, Ecuador, Peru, Bolivia, Chile, and Argentina.

They called themselves Runa, but have become known by the name of their emperor—the Inca.

For the Runa, the Spanish invasion could not possibly have come at a worse time. Their entire empire was centered on the Inca. Only the Inca could choose who would rule after he died, so if the Inca passed away without naming his successor, the empire fell apart. That's what had happened just before Pizarro invaded.

Dying emperor Inca Capac couldn't decide which of his two sons should rule the empire after him. So he said they would each rule half the territory. That was not a good choice, since brothers don't always get along well, especially when great riches and power are at stake. The empire was divided in a bloody *civil* war. One brother, Inca Atahuallpa, had just won and was still finishing off his dead brother's forces when Pizarro marched into Peru.

civil: relating to what happens between different groups of citizens within the same political unit.

Pizarro's Arrival

n November 14, 1532, Pizarro's men had just spent a week hiking over the Andes Mountains. They were exhausted from the high altitude, but Francisco Pizarro had pushed hard to reach the town of Cajamarca. He had heard Inca Atahuallpa was camped there with some of his army.

The Inca emperor met the Spaniards briefly outside of the town and told them to enter the city and wait for him there. Pizarro did so—and took advantage of the wait by hiding men with guns around the meeting place.

renounce: to reject a belief or a claim to something.

blasphemy: something showing disrespect for God or religious ideas and things.

puppet ruler: someone who is in charge of a country in name only; he or she does what someone else, behind the scenes, says to do.

When Inca Atahuallpa arrived, Pizarro, through an interpreter, informed him that the Spanish served a great king who desired the Inca's friendship. Atahuallpa replied that he had no need for friendship with this faraway king, because he was a great ruler in his own empire. Then, Pizarro's priest, Friar Vicente, told the Inca he must *renounce* his idols and believe in God.

The Inca replied he was well satisfied with his own spiritual beliefs, and asked what reasons the Spanish priest had for considering Christian beliefs superior to those of the Incas. Friar Vicente replied that the Word of God (the Bible) spoke to him. Atahuallpa replied, "Give me the book so it can speak to me." He was handed a Bible. Inca Atahuallpa put the Bible up to his ear, listened carefully, then laughingly asked, "Why doesn't the book say anything to me?" He threw it on the ground.

"Blasphemy!" cried Friar Vicente. "Kill them!"

The hidden musketeers fired. Smoke and fire erupted from the walls, thunderous noises echoed across the plaza, and bullets tore through skin, limbs, and hearts of people who had never heard of firearms. The Indians were too astonished to resist. The Spaniards pulled out their swords and began to butcher them. An Inca later recalled, "[The Indians] could not get out, nor did they have any weapons—and the Spanish killed them all just as one would slaughter llamas, for nobody could defend himself."

Inca Atahuallpa was captured. Native women captured in the ambush were raped. Pizarro demanded gold to ransom the emperor. The gold was delivered—seven tons of it—but the Spanish had no intention of setting their hostage free. They attempted to use Inca Atahuallpa as Cortez had used Moctezuma—issuing orders to the Indians from their captive leader. The Peruvian Natives did not fall for this trick. Since

The skill of ancient Inca stone masons amazes the modern world.

their hostage was no longer useful, the Spaniards eventually strangled Inca Atahuallpa.

Following Atahuallpa's death, the Spaniards marched to the capital of Cuzco. They were allowed to enter the city, since it was in large part controlled by Incas who had fought against Atahuallpa in the recent civil war. The conquistadors watched as a new Inca—Manco—was appointed leader over the empire. They assumed Inca Manco would serve them as a *puppet ruler*.

The conquistadors were in for a rude awakening. Shortly after assuming power, Inca Manco met with his top officials. He told them that they must fight against the Spanish for the sake of their empire; then he escaped from Cuzco to organize the Peruvian Indian resistance.

Warfare between the Spaniards and the Inca lasted for forty years, during which time more and more European invaders arrived. While living in hidden cities in the mountains, Inca Manco led raids against the Spanish. Juan Pizarro was killed in battle, and Gonzalo Pizarro took charge of the campaigns against Inca Manco. In 1544, assassins killed Manco, but the Incas fought on for another three decades.

Before he was killed, Inca Manco told his people:

Reflect on how long my ancestors and I have looked after you . . . do not forget us, not in your lifetimes, not in the times of your descendants. Outwardly, you can give the impression of going along with the Europeans' demands. They will make you worship what they worship. When that time comes, when you can no longer resist, do it in front of them, but do not forget our ceremonies. Reveal only what you have to, and keep the rest hidden, close to your hearts.

Even though Spain came to rule Peru, the Incas were not entirely defeated. Their culture still lives today. Quechua (pronounced "kaitch-wa") was the language of the Inca Empire. It is still spoken today by approximately 13 million people in Bolivia, Peru, Ecuador, northern Chile, Argentina, and southern Colombia.

Though outwardly Catholic, the Inca today continue to practice their ancient traditions privately. After four centuries of European rule, their hearts still follow the Inca.

The Maya

 third great empire, that of the Maya, covered Central America and the southern part of Mexico. By the time Europeans arrived, the Maya were less powerful than the Aztecs or the Incas, but they were still able to put up a strong defense of their lands. In 1523, Pedro de Alvarado, Cortez's brutal second-in-command, invaded the Maya in Guatemala.

Attacked by a large European force possessing horses, armor, and guns, the Maya fought bravely with obsidian-tipped darts and leather shields. They suffered terrible losses and became slaves in their own homeland. Their libraries were burned and cities leveled.

Despite this apparent conquest, the majority of Guatemalans today are Mayan Indians, who have preserved their language, heritage, and spiritual beliefs, although they suffer from poverty and *discrimination*.

riven by their unending greed for gold, the conquistadors sent countless expeditions throughout the Americas. To their disappointment, they found no other great kingdoms with abundant gold like the Aztecs and Inca. They did, however, map out large portions of the New World.

discrimination: the unfair treatment of members of one group over those of another group, often based on prejudice.

De Soto

ernando de Soto led a force of six hundred conquistadors through the southeastern quarter of the United States. They marched through lands that are now eleven different states. Though de Soto failed to find any gold, he did manage to enslave, rape, and fight a number of different Indian tribes. Diseases, which came with de Soto's men, wiped out most of the Native population in that part of North America.

Hernando de Soto

Coronado

rancisco Vasquez de Coronado led another group of Spaniards through what are now known as the Great Plains and the southwestern deserts of the United States. He was searching for the legendary Seven Cities of Cibola, which were supposed

A New Capital City

nlike Cortez, Pizarro did not use the Native capital as his capital city. Cuzco, the Inca capital, is today a popular tourist destination—but it is not the capital of Peru. Pizarro first made his capital at Jauja, in the Andes. As war with the Incas continued, he decided he needed to be closer to his ships, so he moved his capital to Lima, which is near the coast. It is said that the conquistadors asked some Incas where they would have good weather for their capital city, and the Incas told them, "Lima—it has plenty of sunshine." In fact, due to an unusual weather phenomenon, Lima is covered with low clouds for most of the year.

adobe: a type of brick made from earth and straw, and dried naturally by the sun.

to be filled with gold. (The cities of Zuni and Acoma, whose *adobe* walls sometimes appear golden when viewed from a distance, may have inspired these rumors.) Coronado took captives and killed a number of peaceful Indians, but he returned from the expedition penniless.

n less than a century, the invasion of South and Central America was largely completed. From the Caribbean Islands to Texas and California, Native people were killed by disease or battle, enslaved, and sexually exploited.

Mansio Serra de Leguizamon was a conquistador who lived longer than most and

The Lost City of the Incas

n 1911, an explorer named Hiram Bingham was hiking along the ancient Inca Trail, in Peru's mountains, looking for historic sites. What he found exceeded his wildest dreams. On a mountain local people called Machu Picchu—which means "Ancient Peak"—he came upon an entire city, still standing, made from enormous stones. He was the first non-Indian to see this breathtaking lost city of the Incas. It contains features of a fortress town, but also a number of religious temples. Today, Machu Picchu is one of the best known and most visited ancient cities in the world.

played a role in many of the famous events of the conquest. In 1589, nearing death, he wrote a letter to Spain's King Philip II:

I wish your Majesty to understand the motive [for this letter] is peace of my conscience because of the guilt I share. For we have destroyed by our evil behavior the government that was enjoyed by these natives. They were so free of crime and greed, both men and women, that they could leave gold or silver worth a hundred thousand pesos in their unlocked house. When they discovered that we were thieves and men who sought to force their wives and daughters to commit sin with them, they despised us. There is nothing more I can do to make right these injustices other than by my words, in which I beg God to forgive me, seeing that I am the last to die of the conquistadors.

The watchtower from Machu Picchu, the Inca's lost city

 abla  spañol

oro (oh-roh): gold

ciudad (see-oo-dahd): city

Dios (dee-ose): God

Pirates of the Carribean

As quickly as the conquistadors stole or mined gold from the New World, it was transported by slaves to the coast and loaded onto ships. A constant stream of wooden-hulled, square-sailed galleons slowly sailed through the Caribbean and back to Spain along the route known as "The Spanish Main." Of course, Spain had enemies in the Old World—most notably the English and French, who were on the opposing side of a religious war. The English and French found there was an easy way to relieve Spain of the New World's treasure—piracy!

Sir Francis Drake, Sir John Hawkins, and other "Sea Rovers" who attacked the galleons and took their gold were heroes in England but hated by the Spaniards. Officially, England's Queen Elizabeth denied giving them permission to raid the Spanish galleons, but privately she praised these English Sea Raiders. Although they served the purposes of their nations, most pirates were motivated to steal from the Spaniards for the same reason the Spaniards stole from the Indians—greed for gold.

Conversion

Am I not here, who am your Mother?

Are you not under my shadow and protection?

Am I not the fountain of your joy?

—words from a miraculous appearance of the Virgin Mary, as told by the Indian peasant Juan Diego, December 1531

oday is December 12. Vast crowds are converging toward the square in front of the *Basilica* de Nuestra Señora de Guadalupe, in the midst of Mexico City. Some have camped out here for nights. Others are arriving by bus, some from countries far away.

Inside the basilica, ten thousand people are gathered. They line up before escalators, which take them underneath the object that has drawn them here. It is a *tilma*, a cape woven from cactus fibers, used by poor American Indians at the time of the conquest. Yet this object is not important just for archaeological or even historical reasons.

On the cape one can see an image of the Virgin Mary. She is dark skinned—clearly an American Indian. For the pilgrims gathered here, her image is evidence of a miracle. Belief in this miracle influenced huge numbers of Mexican Indians to accept Christianity, despite the brutal actions of the Europeans who had previously attempted to convert them. The tilma symbolizes belief in a special appearance of the Virgin Mary, known to Latino Catholics as Our Lady of Guadalupe.

Many people today regard religion as relatively unimportant to their lives or events around them. Things were different, however, at the time of the first contact between the hemispheres. For both the conquistadors and the Natives they encountered, spiritual beliefs ruled every aspect of life. Today, the majority of Latinos are still deeply influenced by spiritual beliefs that took shape in the sixteenth century. To understand the history of Latin America or Latino culture, you need to be familiar with the traditions that surround the Virgin of Guadalupe.

Our Lady of Guadalupe

The Story of Our Lady of Guadalupe

en years after Tenochtitlan fell to Cortez and his Indian allies, a fifty-year-old man named Juan Diego Cuauhtlatoatzin ("Talking Eagle") was walking from his home in Cuauhtitlán to Tlatelolco, in Mexico City, where there was a church. Juan Diego was a Chichimeca Indian of the lower class. As he described himself, "I am really just a man from the country." The walk from Cuauhtitlán to Tlatelolco took more than three hours. On this chilly morning, Juan Diego wore a tilma, or ayate, made with fibers from the maguey cactus.

Cuauhtlatoatzin had always been a deeply spiritual person. Just a few years before, he had met a _Franciscan_ missionary, Friar Toribio de Benavente. The Indians respected Friar

The Virgin of Guadalupe appeared to Juan Diego, as portrayed in this street mural.

Benavente because of his kindness and humility. This caring Spaniard convinced the poor Chichimeca man to believe in the Christian faith. Cuauhtlatoatzin was given the new name "Juan" (after Saint John) and baptized. After his *conversion*, Juan Diego walked fourteen miles every Saturday and Sunday from his home to the nearest church so he could learn more about this new faith.

Catholic American Indians like Juan Diego were unusual at that time. Attempts at conversion had not gone over well. Don Nune de Guzman, who was cruel and ruthless in his treatment of the Indian population, headed the Spanish government of Mexico, known as "the First Audience." He enslaved Native people and branded them on their faces, treating them like cattle. No wonder then that the Native people were not very interested in the Europeans' religion.

Father Juan Zumarraga, the Bishop of Mexico City, was opposed to Guzman and spoke against Governor Guzman's policies. The bishop preached sermons against torturing, killing, and enslaving the Indians. Guzman had Bishop Zumarraga thrown into jail, but the bishop managed to send a message hidden in a crucifix back to Spain. The King of Spain removed the ruthless governor from his office.

A new governor was appointed who treated Native people more fairly. However, the damage was already done. Conquistadors and the First Audience had horribly mistreated Native Americans. As a result, there were few Indians like Juan Diego, who were willing to believe in the conquistadors' religion.

As the story goes, Juan Diego's cold bare feet slapped along the dirt path near a place called Tepeyac, en route to the church in Mexico City. Tepeyac was the site of a shrine to Tonantzin, one of the most important deities worshipped by the Mexica and other Native tribes; Tonantzin means "Our Lady," and she was the mother goddess, identified with the moon.

As he walked along, Juan Diego heard a sound like birds whistling and singing—only more beautiful. The sound was so lovely, he asked himself, "Where am I? Am I possibly in heaven?"

As he came to the top of a hill, he saw a woman. An Aztec document titled *Nican Mopohau* ("It is told"), gives Juan Diego's account of his vision:

> Her clothing was shining like the sun, as if it was sending out rays of light . . . her radiance was like precious stones . . . the earth seemed to shine with the brilliance of a rainbow in the mist.

She was dark skinned—an American Indian, judging from her complexion. Juan Diego fell on his face before the image. She spoke to him in Nahuatl, the Aztec language.

According to tradition, she said to him, "Know for sure, my dearest son, that I am . . . the Virgin Mary, Mother of the One Great God of Truth who gives us life. I am truly your Compassionate Mother, yours and of all the people who live together in this land." She told Juan Diego to build her a

conversion: the changing of someone's beliefs.

"sacred little house" on this site, "because there I will listen to their weeping . . . to remedy, to cleanse and nurse all their different troubles, their miseries, their suffering." She told Juan Diego to deliver her message to Bishop Zumarraga in Mexico City.

Bishop Zumarraga listened politely to the poor Indian, but he did not believe him. Departing from the city for home, Juan Diego again encountered the Virgin. He apologized for his inability to persuade the bishop. He begged her, "Have one of the nobles take your word, so that he will be believed."

She replied, "Listen, my dearest son . . . I have no lack of servants, but it is very necessary that you, personally, go and plead with the bishop."

So Juan Diego again went to Mexico City. Bishop Zumarraga told the Indian he would have to return with some sort of *tangible* proof in order to convince people of this miraculous appearance.

When Juan Diego returned to his home, he found that his uncle was dying. The uncle asked him to hurry and get a priest who could hear his confession before death. En route back to Tlatelolco, Juan Diego again beheld the Virgin. He told her of his uncle's illness. She assured him his uncle was already miraculously healed. Then she told him to fill his tilma with flowers. This seemed odd indeed, for it was the cold season and frost was on the ground. And yet—amazingly—Juan Diego found the place blooming with a great variety of fresh flowers. The Virgin told him to bring the flowers to the Bishop as proof of her appearance.

He went to the city again, and in the Bishop's presence, Juan Diego shook the flowers out of his cape. There on the tilma was the image of the Virgin. Tradition recounts that the image was detailed and lifelike, in bright colors.

The story of The Virgin's appearance to Juan Diego was one of the most important influences that led to the conversion of American Indians in Latin America. Such a miraculous appearance is an account of religious nature, so people of differing backgrounds will understand it in a variety of ways. For Catholics, it is a true miracle. Others view the appearance as a psychological event or a myth. One thing is certain—it has had tremendous impact over the centuries. The Virgin's reported appearance convinced many Native

Americans that the God of the Spaniards was also a deity for the Americas.

Speaking in the Aztec language, the Virgin told Juan Diego her name was Coatlaxopeuh, which is pronounced "Quat-la-su-pay" and sounds similar to the Spanish word *Guadalupe*. Coatlaxopeuh means "One who crushes the serpent." The name echoes a Bible passage found in Genesis 3:15, which Catholics regard as a prophecy of the Virgin Mary. It also had meaning for the Mexica people, who had worshiped the Feathered Serpent god Quetzalcoatl. The Virgin's words imply that worship of Christ would now begin to replace the worship of the Feathered Serpent God. For Spanish speakers, the name Quatlasupe reminded them of Guadalupe, a place in Spain where there was already a shrine dedicated to the Virgin Mary. To this day, this miraculous vision is referred to as the appearance of "Our Lady of Guadalupe."

tangible: something that can be seen or touched.

The Virgin of Guadalupe continues to be popular throughout Hispanic America.

rom the beginning of their invasion, Europeans tried to convert American Indians to the Christian faith. Priests and missionaries came with most of the Spanish expeditions to the New World. The pope had given Spain the right to take all the lands they found—provided they would convert the natives of those lands to Catholicism. The Christianity of the conquistadors had been formed during years of war with the Muslims, so they understood the triumph of their faith in terms of military conflict.

Today, many people find themselves horrified by the conquistadors' brutal mistreatment of the Indians. One may question how a religion that says, "love your neighbor," could be

Christianity played a major role in Hispanic history.

Eucharist: a ceremony in Christian churches in which blessed bread and wine is believed to be transformed into the body and blood of Jesus Christ and is consumed.

used to excuse slavery, slaughter, and rape. Religion can be a powerful force for good in the world, but spiritual beliefs can be horribly misused as well.

Christopher Columbus was convinced God had personally chosen him to sail across the Atlantic to "the Indies." His first name, in Latin, means "Christ bearer," so he believed it was his destiny to bring Christianity to the inhabitants of Asia. Columbus called the place where he first landed Veracruz, which means "the True Cross." After their first encounter, he wrote in his journal that the Natives would make "fine Christians." Sadly, his understanding of religious faith also allowed him to enslave these people and take their land.

Likewise, the conquistadors were, in their misguided way, religious men. Cortez repeatedly attempted to explain Christianity to the Indians he met, before conquering them. He had the custom of celebrating the Christian ceremony of the *Eucharist* before each battle.

Soon after arriving at Tenochtitlan, Cortez was invited by Moctezuma to walk up the steps to the top of the Templo Mayor, the heart of the Mexica spiritual world. At the top of this mountain of white stone, the conquistador was appalled to see human hearts, which had been yanked out of sacrificial victims, set before the image of Huitzilopochtli. He told Moctezuma, "This is a very bad thing," and pressured the Huey Tlatoani to replace his deities with images of Christ and the Virgin. Moctezuma replied that there was nothing wrong with Mexica beliefs; after all, he and his ancestors had worshiped their deities for many years with good results.

Historian Justo Gonzalez comments on encounters between American Indian and Spanish religions: "It was one of the bleakest times in the history of Christianity. In the name of Christ, thousands were slaughtered, millions enslaved, entire

Confess in Hell

rancisco Pizarro was one of the sternest conquistadors. As governor of conquered Peru, he never tried to restrain the brutal treatment of the Inca by his fellow Spaniards. At the end of his life, he became involved in a violent feud between political parties. Mortally wounded, Pizarro made the sign of a cross with his fingers and begged to make a final confession of his sins. His attacker, Juan Barragán, smashed an urn full of water on Pizarro's hand, and shouted, "In Hell—you will have to confess in hell!" Today, Pizarro's bones lie in an elaborate tomb in Lima Cathedral.

civilizations wiped out." Within fifty years, the native population of the Island of Hispaniola was reduced from 100,000 to five hundred. In Mexico, in less than a century, the American Indian population of 23 million was annihilated to only 1.4 million. Likewise, in Peru, in only fifty years, 9 million Incas were reduced to 1.3 million. Devastated by military force, slavery, and disease, it is not surprising that the majority of Native people resisted the conquerors' religious beliefs.

Hatuey, a Caribbean Indian leader, was burned alive at the stake. Before the fire was lit, a Franciscan friar asked him one last time to accept Christianity. He said Hatuey was bound for hell—a place where there would always be torturous flames—if he did not accept the Christian religion before death. He also said if Hatuey would convert, even now, he could go to heaven instead.

Hatuey asked the missionary, "Do Christians go to heaven?"
The friar replied that they did.

Hatuey said, "Then I don't wish to go to heaven, I would rather be in hell so as not to be where the Spaniards are, because I cannot stand to live with such cruel people."

But not all Europeans treated American Indians with such cruelty. Some Spanish religious workers endured considerable hardships to demonstrate compassion to native people. However, their influence was hardly enough to overcome the hurt and mistrust caused by the brutality of the European invasion.

Spanish missionaries realized it would take something extraordinary for great numbers of Indians to believe in Christ. And something unusual did happen. Whole villages of native people accepted Juan Diego's account of the Virgin's appearance. Within a decade, more than 9 million Mexican Natives willingly gave themselves to the Catholic faith.

Today, 90 percent of the people in South America, Central America, and Mexico are Catholic. There are also millions of Latin Americans who have gone from Catholicism to embrace other varieties of Christian faith. Despite the brutality of Christian conquistadors, Latin America today is predominantly committed to the Christian religion. However one explains the appearance of Our Lady of Guadalupe, the effect of her appearance was truly amazing.

Habla Español

padre (pah-dray): father; also used to address a priest of the Catholic Church

fey (fay): faith

religion (ray-lee-hee-own): religion

California, Here We Come

ne way Spanish missionaries tried to evangelize American Indians was the establishment of missions, where Indians could live, be protected, and learn European technical skills. Many of these missions were in what is today the United States. Spain established twenty-five missions in New Mexico and forty-four in Florida. Most famous are the twenty-one missions located along the coast of California, from San Diego all the way up past San Francisco.

These were the work of Miguel José Serra, a Franciscan friar who was fifty-five years old and had a bad limp when he started the first California mission in 1769. Over the next fifteen years, Father Serra baptized more than six thousand Indians.

7

Cries for Justice

You are all in mortal sin,
and live and die in it,
because of the cruelty and tyranny you practice
among these innocent peoples.
Tell me, by what right and what justice
do you hold these Indians
in such a cruel and horrible servitude?
—Antón Montesino, from a sermon he preached in
Hispaniola in 1511

cassava: *a tropical plant with an edible root.*

carnage: *widespread slaughter of people.*

tyrannies: *oppressive governments.*

novel: *new; unique.*

It has been said, "The only thing necessary for the triumph of evil is for good people to say nothing." Even in history's darkest hours, there have been a few who dared to speak against injustice. In the 1500s, a handful of friars in the Dominican religious order preached against the cruel actions of the conquistadors.

Bartolemé de Las Casas

artolemé wiped the sweat off his brow. Perspiration and humidity made his monk's robe cling to his legs and chest, but he was undaunted. Las Casas was thirty years old, thin-faced, with eyes that suggested deep intelligence. He was helping his Indian companions unload packs and place them inside a large thatched-roof hut.

Bartolemé de las Casas

In 1514, las Casas was traveling through Cuba with a large company of Spanish soldiers under the command of Pánfilo de Narváez. They were meeting previously unknown tribes in order to establish trade and explain Christianity to them. The expedition had arrived the previous evening at the town of Caonao. More than two thousand Indians had greeted them here, and served the Spaniards a huge meal of *cassava* bread and fish. This morning, las Casas was away from the troops, helping unload supplies for the Spaniards' stay in the village.

Suddenly, the friar's ears were filled with horrible sounds, screams of pure terror and agonized pain. He ran for the door. Emerging from the shelter, las Casas beheld his worst nightmare. The Spaniards were massacring their hosts.

As las Casas later recalled, the soldiers proceeded "to rip open their bellies, to cut and kill those lambs—men, women, children, and old folks." Indians fled in every direction. Some tried to hide, others fled toward the jungle, and others attempted to climb atop their houses. On horse and on foot, the soldiers pursued, and the *carnage* continued.

Captain Narváez sat on his horse, holding his lance and calmly presiding over the slaughter. Seeing the shocked look on the friar's face, he asked Bartolomé, "How does your honor like what our men have done?"

The clergyman, in his horror and disgust, choked out his reply, "You and your men can go to the devil!"

Before this, las Casas had not protested his countrymen's mistreatment of Native people. As a missionary to the Indians, he cared for them deeply. Yet he owned an *encomienda* (ranch) with Indian slaves. But the massacre at Caonao forced him to rethink his beliefs. Las Casas freed all his Indian slaves.

Sometime later, he preached in a church at a place called Espiritu Santo (Holy Spirit), on a festival day when many Spaniards were gathered there. He delivered a message "to declare the injustices, *tyrannies*, and cruelties they were committing . . . how they could not be saved while holding Indians [as slaves]." Las Casas described the reaction of the people who heard this sermon:

> All were astonished . . . hearing something so *novel* as a declaration that they could not, without being considered sinners, possess Indians. They did not believe it, as if it were said that they could not make use of the beasts of the field.

Las Casas continued to preach against mistreatment of the Native people, but without good results. He realized he would have to take his concerns to higher authorities. He sailed back to Spain, where he insisted on speaking to officials in the church and in the government; he also wrote letters and books. His activities earned him the title "Protector of the Indians." For decades, he labored in the Old World, reporting abuses against Indians, and in the New World, as a missionary and as a bishop.

Other Catholic priests, like Antonio Montesinos, defended the rights of the Native people.

Finally, in 1550, las Casas' unceasing efforts were taken seriously. King Charles V ordered that all Spanish conquests of Native Americans be halted until a debate could be held on the subject. In July and September 1550, a commission of experts on religion and law were gathered in Valladolid, Spain, to hear arguments on the rights of American Indians. In the history of Europe, this was the first serious discussion of universal human rights.

Juan Ginés de Sepúlveda argued against Indians' rights. He was the official historian for the Spanish monarchy. Sepulveda had never met an American Indian and had never been to the New World. He began his argument stating:

> The man rules over the woman, the adult over the child. . . .
> That is to say, the most powerful and perfect rule over the
> weakest and most imperfect. There are some who by nature are
> masters and others who by nature are slaves.

He went on to argue that Indians are "barbarous and inhuman peoples who have no civil life and no peaceful customs." For such inferior beings, he argued, it is "merciful" for them to be conquered and forced to serve "civilized" people.

Bartolemé de las Casas argued against Sepúlveda, combining his firsthand knowledge of American Indians with brilliant legal arguments. He explained how the Spanish conquests turned Native people against the beliefs of their invaders:

> If *pagans* find themselves injured, oppressed, saddened and
> afflicted by . . . wars, loss of their children, their goods, and

A Voice Crying in the Wilderness

lthough las Casas was the greatest defender of Indian rights, he was not the first. In 1511, Dominican friar Antonio de Montesinos shocked his listeners in a sermon delivered at a church in Hispaniola. He was speaking on a Bible reference found in Matthew 5:3, "a voice crying in the wilderness." He told his listeners their conscience was as lifeless as a desert. He declared himself the voice of God, "to let you know of your sins." He catalogued the ways they mistreated Native people, "you kill them, so that you may obtain more and more gold." He told them they would certainly not go to heaven if they continued to mistreat the Indians.

Colonists who heard of this speech were furious. They threatened Montesinos and the priests who agreed with him. They sent letters of protest to King Ferdinand and church officials in Spain. Letters were sent back, ordering the Dominicans to apologize. Against the orders of their King and their church, the priests stood fast to their beliefs. Antonio de Montesinos was the first European to protest on behalf of American Indian rights.

their liberty . . . how can they listen to what is told them about faith, religion, justice and truth.

He also argued for universal human rights, "The entire human race is one; all men are alike."

Las Casas did succeed in getting laws passed to protect the rights of American Indians. Unfortunately, these laws written in Spain were not taken seriously in the New World. They were largely broken and ignored—but they did have some influence. Without the efforts of this compassionate and determined man, the sad history of Spain's invasion of the Americas might have been even worse. Furthermore, Las Casas's defense of universal human rights helped create the ideals that all nations in the Americas aspire to today.

Cabeza de Vaca

nother European who championed Indian rights was Alvar Núñez Cabeza de Vaca. One of the most fascinating stories in the history of the Americas is contained in his book, *The Journey and Ordeal of Cabeza de Vaca*. Cabeza de Vaca's adventures might remind modern readers of the movie *Dances with Wolves,* except that his story is true—and even more amazing than fiction.

Cabeza de Vaca was a member of an expedition led by Pamfilo de Narváez, the same man who commanded the massacre at Caonao. Narváez set out to explore the southeastern regions of what is today North America. Anything that could go wrong with the expedition did.

A Spanish postage stamp commemorates Cabeza de Vaca.

Slave of the Slaves

edro Claver was a Jesuit missionary who declared himself "slave to the Negroes." He was born into a wealthy family. At the age of thirty, he traveled to Colombia where he saw ships full of African slaves being unloaded. The ships' holds were piled with naked bodies, some dead and covered with flies. Claver was shocked into action. He provided slaves with food, clothing, and medical care. For the rest of his life, Claver worked tirelessly for their betterment, causing his own health to suffer as a result.

After a storm, Cabeza de Vaca and a handful of men found themselves cast ashore, naked and starving, on an island off the coast of Texas. A group of Indians found them and carried them on their backs to a village. Cabeza de Vaca and his companions, having heard stories of Mexican Indian practices, feared they were about to be offered as sacrifices. Instead, the Indians fed and clothed them. Over time, as the Europeans lived with the tribe, they learned the Indians' language.

One day, Cabeza de Vaca writes, "The islanders wanted to make physicians of us." A shaman demanded that Cabeza de Vaca heal a sick man. He replied that he was not a doctor, but the Indian insisted. Cabeza de Vaca proceeded to make a sign of blessing over the

Cabeza de Vaca is remembered for planting his cross at the summit of Sierrita de la Santa Cruz.

Cabeza de Vaca in captivity

sick man, breathed on him, and prayed "earnestly" for his recovery. The sick man got up and announced himself healed!

Over the next several years, Cabeza de Vaca and his companions managed to walk across Texas and down the center of northern Mexico, a journey of 2,500 miles, until they reached Mexico City. They learned eight different native languages and adapted themselves to the ways of a variety of Indian cultures. In all the lands where they journeyed, they were the first white men seen. Along the way, hundreds of sick or injured people requested them to pray for healing. Cabeza de Vaca's journal and oral traditions, told among Mexican Indians even today, record an amazing number of cures attributed to Cabeza de Vaca and his friends.

When they finally reached the area of Mexico City, Cabeza de Vaca was appalled at what he saw. Entire villages had been destroyed, and whole tribes were captured as slaves. A group of Indians had accompanied Cabeza de Vaca on his long walk, and these Indians refused to believe that Cabeza de Vaca and his friends were actually the same race as other Europeans. Cabeza de Vaca recalls the words of his Indian companions:

> We [Cabeza de Vaca and friends] healed sick people, they [other Spaniards] killed healthy people, we came naked and barefoot, they came with clothes, horses and weapons; we were not greedy but gave away gifts we were given, while they robbed whomever they found and gave away nothing.

Cabeza de Vaca returned to Spain and begged for authority over one of the colonies so he could defend the rights of the Native inhabitants. He was allowed to do so, but his pro-Indian policies infuriated other European colonists. They made up false charges against him, and Cabeza de Vaca was sent back to Spain for sentencing. For many years, he was involved in legal battles that drained him financially and emotionally.

Although he failed in his political attempts to help the American Indians, Cabeza de Vaca nonetheless played an important role in the history of the Americas. He was the first European to live among Native American people, then return to European society and write about his experiences. Through his written accounts, Europeans could glimpse the common humanity they shared with the Native people of the Americas.

artolemé de las Casas, Alvar Núñez Cabeza Cabeza de Vaca, and others like them had the rare courage to go against the crowd when they saw injustice. They were some of the first Europeans to join with Native people in their struggle for fair treatment. In countries throughout North, South, and Central America, that struggle continues today.

Don't Miss the DVD

f this chapter interests you, don't miss a movie titled *The Mission*. It portrays Jesuit missionaries who struggled to defend American Indians in Brazil, in the early 1700s, against the greed and brutality of other Europeans. It may sadden—or infuriate—you, but it brings this historic period powerfully to life.

paz (pahs): peace

justicia (hoo-stees-ee-ah): justice

amigos (ah-mee-goes): friends

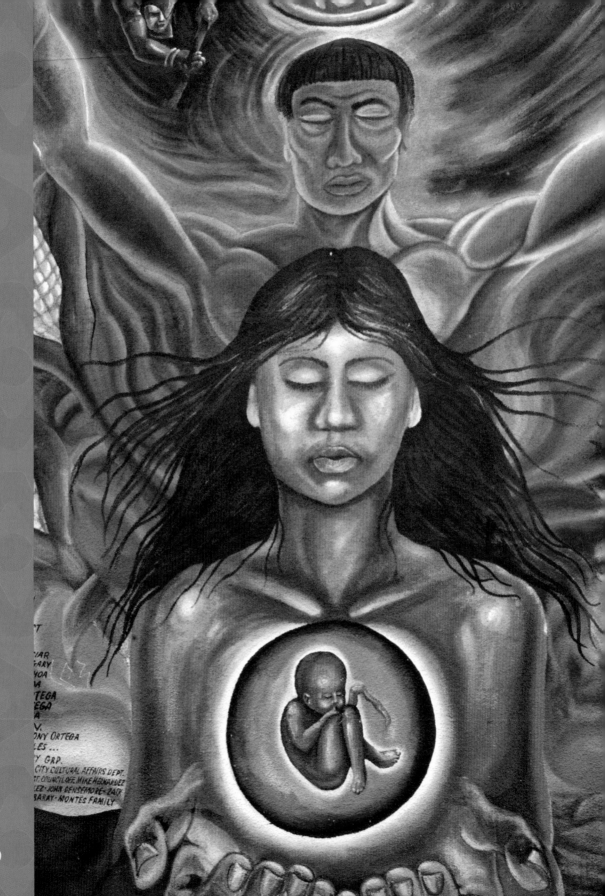

8

Colonization and the Birth of La Raza

Jaime Gonzales lets his mom kiss him on the cheek as he heads out the door—it's a tad embarrassing in front of his friends, but she's done it all his life, and he figures she'll keep doing it as long they're both alive. He knows that he's lucky to have parents who care for him so much, so he doesn't mind his mom doting on him.

Artwork

A street mural in Los Angeles portrays the birth of the Latino people.

Modern Latino youth struggle with many issues.

He jumps into his friend Enrique's car—a metallic blue '78 Olds Cutlass. As they pull away from the curb, Jaime, Enrique, and Enrique's girlfriend Xochitl argue over the CDs they want to hear. Jaime likes rock music—he wants to play U2—but Xochitl and Enrique want to listen to tejano—Latino music from Texas, with more of a country sound. Jaime gives in on the music, and they talk about the big game against Huntington Park High on Friday night and about the test that day in global history. Xochitl is all studied up, but Enrique had to help his dad install a Jacuzzi, so he hasn't hit the books as much as he should have.

Jaime and his friends talk about things that are important to high school kids in 2005. Sometimes, though, Jaime and his parents think back to their ancestors and the great historical events that have brought them to this place and time. The Gonzaleses are descendants of Mexica Indians who migrated from Aztlan a thousand years ago, who helped build the great city of Tenochtitlan. They are also descended from conquistadors who came from Castile and warred against the Aztecs.

The first generation of children with European and American Indian heritage were called mestizos. This term became less important over time, so Jaime's great-grandparents simply thought of themselves as Mexicanos. Their children—Jaime's grandparents—moved to San Diego in the 1920s and helped build homes as southern California grew. His parents moved further north to Los Angeles, where his mom works as an interior designer and his dad is an engineer.

In the 1970s, Jaime's parents gained a new sense of pride in their identity. They came to see themselves as members of La Raza—the new race, born out of the fusion of peoples inhabiting the Americas.

La Raza

s they invaded and gained control of the Americas, Europeans focused on ways to exploit the New World for the benefit of the Old. They pillaged all the metals they could find, melted precious works of art into silver and gold ingots, and sent them back to Spain in ships so weighed down that some of them sank from the weight of their cargoes. Soon they had stripped the native peoples of their valuables, and turned to the more difficult task of mining precious metals. This was hard work, and slaves were imported from Africa to do the labor, alongside enslaved Indians.

The African slave trade would play an indispensable role in the European settlement and development of the New World. By 1750, slaves were owned, bought, and sold throughout the American colonies. In fact, the number of Africans taken by force to the Western Hemisphere was actually greater than the number of Europeans who came to the Americas in all the years before 1800! Between 1492 and 1820, between 10 and 15 million Africans were taken captive, packed into foul compartments below the decks of slave ships, and sold for labor in the Americas. They were often captured and forced into slavery by other Africans, who engaged in the slave trade in exchange for trade goods and military support from the European nations.

Conquistadors soon realized the value of the Western Hemisphere, not only as a source of exported wealth, but as land to be colonized. There was not a great amount of farmland available in Spain. Queen Isabella, with her mind for administration, established what became known as the encomienda system—after the Spanish word for something given in trust. Each encomienda was a combination plantation and mission. The Spanish Crown granted each conquistador ownership of a parcel of land in the Americas, along with the right to force the inhabitants of that land to work for them. In exchange for their work, the owner was expected to "care for" the Indians and teach them Christianity. In reality, the owners abused their Indian workers more than they cared for them.

Las Casas and others fought for the abolishment of the encomienda system—and to some degree lessened its harmful effects. At the same time, the colonization of the

Día de La Raza

Throughout the Americas, October 12 (or the nearest Monday) is traditionally celebrated as the day Christopher Columbus reached the New World in 1492. While some rightly recall the tragic mistreatment of American Indians and Africans that followed Columbus's arrival, the day is nonetheless celebrated. It is referred to as "Día de La Raza"—"Day of the Race." It is not a celebration of Columbus as an individual, but a celebration of the multicultural, multiethnic society that has come to characterize the Americas today.

Americas—and the mutual needs of its European and Native inhabitants—led to the intermingling of a variety of races.

There's a saying, "Columbus landed in 1492, and nine months later the first latinoamericano was born." From the first contact, Europeans had sexual relationships with Native Americans. Cortez and Pizarro both had children by Indian partners. In many cases, pregnancies were the result of rapes, but there were also lasting and tender unions between the races. Despite the ways Europeans mistreated Africans and Indians, the diverse peoples living in the New World recognized their need for one another.

In colonial times, the people of Latin America were segregated according to their race—Spanish, Indian, African, mulatto (a mixture of African and European), mestizo (a mixture of European and Indian), and so on. Over time, however, these definitions became less and less important.

In the 1800s, the colonies of Spain and Portugal declared their independence from the Old World. People thought of themselves less as Spanish, Indian, or African, and more as citizens of the American nations.

Today, Latino people are a growing and important part of the populations in the United States and Canada, as well as in Latin America. Latinos are making vital contributions in politics, business, science, the arts, and religion. Few Latinos are descended purely from one particular racial background; they do not consider such issues important. Native American, Castilian, and African ancestries have merged to form a new kind of people.

In Mexico City, there is a place called the Plaza of Three Cultures. It is located at the site of the Mexica's final battle against Cortez and his soldiers. A plaque there reads, "Neither a victory nor a defeat, but the painful birth of the Mexico of today, of a race of Mestizos."

Hispanics or Latinos?

Both terms are commonly used to refer to people of multiracial heritage, originating from Spanish-speaking countries. The word "Hispanic" was invented by English speakers, and has been used for a century now to refer to people somehow connected with Spain. The word "Latino" is from the Spanish language. Spanish nouns have gender attached to the ending—so a "Latino" is a man, and a woman is a "Latina." These terms are preferred by an increasing number of people, for several reasons. "Latino" connects someone's heritage to Latin America, rather than Spain. It is a term that comes from within the Latino community, rather than being imposed by an outside agency (the U.S. Census Bureau uses the term "Hispanic").

Many regrettable things have happened in the history of the Americas, but the whole world continues to be blessed by the contributions of Latino people—a new race that came into being from the meeting of two worlds.

Habla Español

raza (rah-sah): race

día (dee-ah): day

gente (hane-tay): people

Timeline

250–900—Mayas develop an advanced civilization.

1200–1500—Mexicas (Aztec) Empire formed in Mexico.

1325—The Mexicas establish their capital at Teneochtitlan.

1438–1532—Incas expand their empire.

1469—Princess Isabella of Castille and Prince Ferdinand of Aragon marry.

October 12, 1492—Christopher Columbus arrives in the Indies.

1492–1820—Between 10 and 15 million Africans are captured, brought to the Americas, and sold as slaves.

1517—Martin Luther sets the stage for the Reformation.

1519—Hernando Cortéz's fleet lands on the Mexican coast.

December 1520—Cortéz and his men conquer the Aztec Empire (with the help of small-pox).

1523—Pedro de Alvarado invades the Mayas in Guatemala.

December 1531—The Virgin Mary (Our Lady of Guadelupe) appears to Juan Diego near Mexico City.

November 14, 1532—Francisco Pizarro and his men encounter the Incas.

1544—Inca ruler Manco is assassinated.

1550—King Charles V orders all Spanish conquests of Native Americans to halt.

1769—Miguel José Serra, a Franciscan friar, establishes the first mission in California.

Further Reading

Bleeker, Sonia. *The Aztec Indians of Mexico*. New York: William Morrow, 1993.

Boone, Elizabeth Hill. *The Aztec World*. Toronto: St. Remy Press, 1994.

Bradford, Ernle. *Christopher Columbus*. New York: Viking Press, 1993.

Cabeza de Vaca, Alvar Núñez. *The Journey and Ordeal of Cabeza de Vaca*. Mineola, N.Y.: Dover, 2003.

Culbert, Patrick. *Maya Civilization*. Toronto: St. Remy Press, 1993.

Editors of Time-Life Books. *Aztecs: Reign of Blood and Splendor*. Alexandria, Va.: Time-Life Books, 1992.

Figueredo, D. H. *Latino History and Culture*. Indianapolis, Ind.: Alpha Books, 2002.

Innes, Hammond. *The Conquistadors*. New York: Alfred A. Knopf, 1999.

Morrison, Samuel Eliot. *Admiral of the Ocean Sea: A Life of Christopher Columbus*. Boston: Little, Brown & Company, 1992.

Morrison, Eliot Samuel. *The Great Explorers*. New York: Oxford University Press, 1998.

Prescott, William H. *The World of the Incas*. Geneva, Switzerland: Minerva, 1990.

Sanderlin, George, ed. *Witness: Writings of Bartolomé de Las Casas*. Maryknoll, N.Y.: Orbis Books, 1991.

Thomas, Hugh. *Conquest: Montezuma, Cortés, and the Fall of Old Mexico*. New York: Simon & Schuster, 1993.

Tsouras, Peter G. *Warlords of the Ancient Americas*. London: Arms and Armour Press, 1996.

Wood, Michael. *Conquistadors*. Berkeley: University of California Press, 2000.

For More Information

Civilizations in America—the Mexica and
Aztecs
www.wsu.edu/~dee/CIVAMRCA/AZTE
CS.HTM

La Malinche—Harlot or Heroine? (article
by Shep Lenchek)
www.mexconnect.com/mex_/history/mal-
inche.html

Columbus and the Age of Discovery
muweb.millersville.edu/~columbus/

Las Culturas (an outstanding resource for
all things Latino)
www.lasculturas.com/

Christopher Columbus Articles (origi-
nally published in VISTA magazine)
www.flmnh.ufl.edu/anthro/caribarch/
columbus.htm

Publisher's note:

The Web sites listed on this page were active at the time of publication. The publisher is
not responsible for Web sites that have changed their addresses or discontinued operation
since the date of publication. The publisher will review the Web sites and update the list
upon each reprint.

Index

Biographies

Kenneth McIntosh is a freelance writer and former educator. His wife, Marsha, is also a former educator and most recently worked with foreign college students. They recently moved from upstate New York to Flagstaff, Arizona, near the Navajo and Hopi reservations. Kenneth has been interested in American Indian cultures since childhood. He spent the summer of his junior year in college volunteering with native youth on a reservation in British Columbia. For this series, both Kenneth and Marsha traveled to Indian nations around the United States, listening and learning.

Dr. José E. Limón is professor of Mexican-American Studies at the University of Texas at Austin, where he has taught for twenty-five years. He has authored over forty articles and three books on Latino cultural studies and history. He lectures widely to academic audiences, civic groups, and K–12 educators.

Picture Credits

Benjamin Stewart: pp. 11, 16, 17, 85, 101, 102

Benjamin Stewart, Museum of Spanish Colonial Art, Sante Fe, New Mexico: pp. 78, 79

Benjamin Stewart, Sanctuario de Chimayo: pp. 48, 81

Corbis: p. 45

Corel: pp. 9, 25, 71, 76, 90

Dover: p. 54

NASA: p. 42

PhotoDisc: p. 54

Photos.com: p. 68

The Ruth M. Reynolds Papers, Centro de Estudios Puertorriqueños, Hunter College, CUNY, Photographer unknown: 91